# EXTRAORDINARY
# FAITH

# OTHER BOOKS BY SHEILA WALSH

*All That Really Matters*
*A Love So Big: Anchoring Your Child to the Heart of God*
*The Heartache No One Sees*
*God Has a Dream for Your Life*
*I'm Not Wonder Woman*
*Living Fearlessly*
*Stories from the River of Mercy*
*Stones from the River of Mercy*
*Life Is Tough but God Is Faithful*
*Gifts for Your Soul*
*Honestly*
*Bring Back the Joy*

## CHILDREN'S BOOKS

*Gigi, God's Little Princess*
*Gigi, God's Little Princess #2: The Royal Tea Party*
*Gigi, God's Little Princess #3: The Perfect Christmas Gift*
*Gigi, God's Little Princess #4: The Pink Ballerina*
*Will, God's Mighty Warrior #1: Will, God's Mighty Warrior*
*Will, God's Mighty Warrior #2: The Mystery of Magillicuddy's Gold*
*God's Little Princess Devotional Bible*
*God's Mighty Warrior Devotional Bible*
*In Search of the Great White Tiger* (#1 in the Gnoo Zoo series)
*Chattaboonga's Chilling Choice* (Gnoo Zoo #2)
*Einstein's Enormous Error* (Gnoo Zoo #3)
*Miss Marbles's Marvelous Makeover* (Gnoo Zoo #4)
*Big Billy's Great Adventure* (Gnoo Zoo #5)
*Hello, Sun! A Morningtime Tale of God's Great Care*
*Hello Stars! A Sleepytime Tale of God's Loving Presence*

## COAUTHORED WOMEN OF FAITH® BOOKS

*Women of Faith® Devotional Bible*
*The Great Adventure*
*Irrepressible Hope*
*Sensational Life*
*The Women of Faith® Daily Devotional*
*The Women of Faith® Study Guide Series*

# EXTRAORDINARY
# FAITH

GOD'S PERFECT GIFT *for* EVERY WOMAN'S HEART

# SHEILA WALSH

THOMAS NELSON
*Since 1798*

NASHVILLE   DALLAS   MEXICO CITY   RIO DE JANEIRO   BEIJING

Published in Nashville, Tennessee. Thomas Nelson is a trademark of Thomas Nelson, Inc.

Published in association with Yates & Yates, LLP, Attorneys and Counselors, Orange, California.

Thomas Nelson, Inc. titles may be purchased in bulk for educational, business, fundraising, or sales promotional use. For information, please email SpecialMarkets@ThomasNelson.com.

### Library of Congress Cataloging-in-Publication Data

Walsh, Sheila.
    Extraordinary faith : God's perfect gift for every woman's heart /
Sheila Walsh.
      p. cm.
        ISBN 10: 0-8499-1856-1 (trade paper)
        ISBN 13: 978-0-8499-1856-8 (trade paper)
        ISBN 10: 0-7852-6291-1 (hardcover)
        ISBN 13: 978-0-7852-6291-6 (hardcover)
    1. Christian women—Religious life. 2. Faith. I. Title.
BV4527.W349 2005
234'.23—dc22

                    2004027612

*Printed in the United States of America*

07 08 09 10 11 RRD 9 8 7 6 5 4 3 2 1

*This book is dedicated
with love and gratitude to
Gilbert Kirby, whose life
has illumined my path.*

# Contents

❧

# An Introduction

⟡

*W*ord quickly spread through the small English village that a healing evangelist would be holding a crusade on Friday night in the village hall. People met the news with both great excitement and skepticism. Some members of the small church on the corner of Elm and Main thought it a disgrace, believing that faith healings did not take place anymore, while others were curious, even hopeful—none more so than Tom.

For as long as he could remember, Tom had been plagued by a stutter. It made social conversation very difficult. He was fine when he was hanging out at home; he could be exceedingly verbose with his cat. But whenever he found himself in a situation with another human being, it was as if his words became backed up like a traffic jam on market day.

Tom's best friend was Sammy, and Sammy had an impediment of his own. Due to an unfortunate event at a soccer game in high school, something he referred to only as "The day the ball went one way and I went the other," his right knee would not hold his weight. Sammy used one crutch and thus limped his way through life. Tom and Sammy decided that on Friday night they would be at the village hall in plenty of time to get good seats for the crusade.

The evening arrived and the small hall was packed to capacity, with Tom and Sammy right in the center of the front row. After a few announcements of upcoming village events, the local vicar welcomed the evangelist to the platform. At first sight he was a little disappointing. It was obvious to most that he was wearing a rather bad toupee. Tom decided that it looked like a tired gerbil or something borrowed from Mr. Potato Head. The evangelist spoke for what was only twenty minutes but seemed like an hour, then invited anyone who was expecting a miracle that night to come up onto the platform. Tom and Sammy shot to their feet and with the help of an usher were soon right beside the evangelist.

"There must be more," he said. "Is no one else expecting a miracle tonight, O ye of little faith?"

Mrs. Trotter considered going up for prayer for her bunions but decided the excitement might be too much for her. Anyway she had an appointment with the chiropodist next Tuesday.

"Very well, then," the evangelist said. "Just these two brothers will receive their miracles this evening!"

"We're not brothers," Sammy whispered. The evangelist ignored him.

The guest speaker then asked an assistant to bring a large screen that had been off to one side into the center of the stage. He positioned it in front of Tom and Sammy, obscuring them from the audience. He moved in front of the screen and announced to the crowd, "Now you will see what faith can do. Sammy, throw away your crutch!"

There was a loud bang that woke Mr. Trotter.

The evangelist continued, "Tom, say something!"

After a long pause, Tom said, "S-s-s-s-sammmmy's f-f-f-allen over!"

One of my theology professors told me that little story when I was a student in London. I thought it was very funny and also a little sad—poor Sammy! He went on to explain that when we graduated and were set loose on an unsuspecting public, we would encounter many things in the name of faith. He reminded us that the church is divided denominationally and experientially.

"Some of you will go on to become pastors. One of the challenges will be to keep your faith when life becomes difficult, and your congregation is no longer as enamored with you as when you started. Some will expect you to represent God, and others will expect you to *be* God—but that position is already filled. Good day!"

With that he left a classroom full of students with more questions than they had at the beginning of the lesson. My number one question was, *What does God expect from me?* And then, *What does it mean to keep the faith? What is faith? How do I guard against losing my faith?*

After I graduated I encountered many circumstances and events that seemed ridiculous to me, and all supposedly took place in the name of *faith.* The most absurd event happened in a small church in England that had experienced a fresh touch of God's presence. One young man had set his heart upon becoming a prophet—I'll call him Jim. Jim could think of nothing more fulfilling than bringing the very words of the living God to His people. He had asked one of the elders, apparently, how to go about becoming a prophet and had been told to trust God and just open his mouth.

On one particular Sunday morning, he determined that he would begin to exercise his new calling that day! The church youth group had organized a barbecue and barn dance the previous evening to raise funds for a summer mission trip. It had been a great success, and Jim wanted to encourage the young people in their efforts. There was a brief pause in the worship, and Jim took it as a sign. He rose to his feet and said, "Thus says the Lord, 'I had a great time last night. In fact, I haven't enjoyed Myself so much since I parted the Red Sea!'" (A true story!)

I'd love to tell you that Jim quit there, but on another occasion he rose to his feet and said, "As I said through my servant Paul in Ephesians chapter six, 'Make every effort to keep the unity of the Spirit through the bond of peace.' Amen." He sat down. A few moments later he rose once more. "This is the Lord again. I beg your pardon—it was Ephesians chapter four."

After that someone in the church had a little word with Jim and redirected his steps. I'm sure his heart and motives were pure, but the idea that the almighty Creator of heaven and earth messed up a Scripture reference made my toes curl. Jim's defense was that he was stepping out in faith.

If you were asked to define *faith,* I wonder what would come to mind. I've heard the word used in many different contexts. At times it is used to condemn what appears to be lack of faith:

"If I'd had more faith, my husband would have come back to me."
"She didn't get healed because she didn't have enough faith."
"O ye of little faith!"
"Where is your faith?"

At times the word is used to encourage or make a statement about our attitude:

"Keep the faith!"
"I've got the faith for it!"
"She's a real woman of faith!"

When we turn the beam onto God, our Father, we are familiar with statements such as

"Great is Thy faithfulness!"
"God is faithful, and He will do it!"

Faith can be defined as *confidence, trust, assurance, conviction, belief.* Webster defines faith as "belief and trust in and loyalty to God."

I conducted a search through *Encyclopedia Britannica,* one of my favorite research tools, to see what it had to offer. The Greek word for *faith* is *pistis;* the Latin is *fidis,* the root for the word *fidelity.* According to the encyclopedia, in Christian theology faith is "the divinely inspired human response to God's historical revelation through Jesus Christ and, consequently, is of crucial significance."

I found it interesting that when the encyclopedia compared all the major religions of the world, Christianity and Judaism were the only ones that continually combined *faith* with religion. Many of the other religions of the world combined *duty* or *works* with religion.

I asked the young Vietnamese girl who does my nails what the word *faith* meant to her. At first she was unsure what I was asking. I told her that I was aware that the girls in the salon prepared a bowl of fruit and set it in front of a small effigy of Buddha. She said they did that for protection and out of respect, for good luck. I asked her if she talked to Buddha, and she gave me one of her big smiles and said something I have heard from her many times: "Miss Sheila, you crazy!"

When we study faith in the biblical context, it has both an active and a passive sense. In an active sense, faith is our loyalty and devotion to God; in a passive sense, our resting confidence in God, in His Word, and in His promises.

Faith is not just *what* we believe, our doctrine or denominational creed, but also and more importantly, a rock-solid conviction that what we believe and *whom we believe in* are worth staking our lives on; they are real and living.

Christian faith is more than wishful thinking; it is a certainty, a constant assurance based on God's track record in our lives and the lives of the faithful through the generations. It's my prayer that as we look at faith together, we will come to a crystal clear resting place at the end of our journey that our world, the church, and our own lives are filled with overwhelming evidence of the faithfulness of God.

I love how *The Expository Dictionary* defines faith.

People today may use "faith" to indicate what is possible but uncertain. The Bible uses "faith" in ways that link it with what is assuredly and certainly true. Christians may sometimes speak of "believing," as if it were merely a subjective effort, as if our act of faith or strength of faith were the issue. But the Bible shifts our attention from subjective experience and centers it on the object of our faith—God himself.

When I began writing this book, I was concerned that what I wrote might make readers who are already stretched to the limit with commitments feel more pressure than ever. Would the call to *Extraordinary Faith* be a clarion call to do more? As I continued to write, one thing became crystal clear to me, from the opening words of the book of Genesis to the triumphant end of the Revelation to John: God's Word is all about His faithfulness to us even when we are faithless! I am convinced, won over, sure, persuaded, and certain that faith is not about what we are able to muster up; it is indeed all about God's faithfulness revealed through Jesus. Charles Haddon Spurgeon wrote, "It is not thy hold on Christ that saves thee; it is Christ. It is not thy joy in Christ that saves thee; it is Christ. It is not even thy *faith* in Christ that saves thee, though that be the instrument. It is Christ's blood and merit."

Spurgeon stated that even in the arena of salvation our faith is simply an instrument of access to what Christ has already finished. I now define faith as *my soul's fixed, unflinching gaze on Christ, wherever that takes me.*

Writing this book has been quite an adventure. Everything that could have gone wrong did go wrong. That seemed no accident to me but a gift from God to keep my gaze on Jesus and shake up any easy interpretation of what a life of faith looks like. As Eliza E. Hewitts hymn says,

> I need no other argument,
> I need no other plea,
> It is enough that Jesus died,
> And that He died for me.
> ("My Faith Has Found a Resting Place")

I don't know what you are expecting from a book on faith. Perhaps you picked it up imagining that I would give you a list of things to do to transform your faith from ordinary to extraordinary. I have often been drawn to a book title because I recognize a lack in my own life. When I was in my twenties, my shelves were filled with books on the subject of prayer. I felt very inadequate in my prayer life, and I wanted someone to tell me how to change that. Perhaps that's where you find yourself today as you consider that idea of faith.

We live in uncertain times in our country and across the world, and you may find yourself longing for a faith that will withstand whatever lies ahead. I long for that too. As a young woman I imagined that living a life of faith meant that I needed to do more, believe more, be more. I lived under a self-inflicted mandate to bolster my faith, to make a new commitment to be more faithful or exercise more faith, but what I have been gifted with in recent years is a new understanding of the depth of God's faithfulness in every situation in life.

In the following pages we will meet many people who will talk to us about what it means to live by faith. Some died centuries ago, but their words and wisdom are fresh and alive; some walk this earth with us now. You will also meet two friends of mine: one is living in the most difficult days of her life; the other, in the most miraculous. They both love God and are committed to Him, but their prayers are being answered very differently. As we listen to the stories of those who walked the earth centuries ago and those who walk with us today, I believe we will see a pattern. It's a pattern that weaves through the lives of both those who received the answers they prayed for and those who received the answers they dreaded: God's faithfulness shines through each one.

I firmly believe that as we study God's Word and His ways together, we will be changed.

So let's begin!

# CHAPTER I

# AN UNCERTAIN BEGINNING

## *When Our Plans Fall Apart*

∽

*My faith has found a resting place,*
*Not in device or creed;*
*I trust the ever living One,*
*His wounds for me shall plead.*
*I need no other argument,*
*I need no other plea,*
*It is enough that Jesus died,*
*And that He died for me.*
                    —Eliza E. Hewitt, 1891

*Now faith is the substance of things hoped for,*
*the evidence of things not seen.*
                    —Hebrews 11:1 NKJV

*I*t's Friday, June 11, 2004. It's a night I will never forget. It's a night forever seared into the hearts and minds of a nation, whether Republican or Democrat, for tonight Ronald Wilson Reagan's body was buried by the ocean he loved in Southern California.

It has been an amazing week of ceremony, celebration, grief, and reflection. Each time the flag-draped casket appeared, a military band struck up the anthem "Hail to the Chief." The body was transported from the funeral home to the Reagan library, to Andrews Air Force Base, to the majesty and quiet reverence of the Capitol building, to a glorious service in the Washington Cathedral, and finally home again to rest in the West. A nation and a world watched an eighty-two-year-old widow, fragile yet steely with love, do the last thing she could do for her beloved Ronnie. My husband Barry and I watched it all, often with tears rolling down our faces. We loved and admired this man. To me he represented all that I, as a young woman growing up in Scotland, appreciated about America. I loved his smile and his charm. I respected his unabashed love of his country and people. I loved his kindness. I loved that perhaps above all else, for it can be a rare commodity in our world.

Reagan was a powerful man and yet, as many observed, he seemed to wear his power lightly. It was crystal clear to all who knew him that he loved his wife passionately. Today, as she leaned on the arm of Major General Galen B. Jackman, Nancy Reagan looked so alone. Even in a crowded cathedral, surrounded by family and friends, she looked alone.

The eulogies offered this morning were tender, profound, and full of faith. Baroness Margaret Thatcher's words made me weep with joy. She said,

> For the final years of his life, Ronnie's mind was clouded by illness. That cloud has now lifted. He is himself again—more himself than at any time on this earth. For we may be sure that the Big Fella Upstairs never forgets those who remember Him. And as the last journey of this faithful pilgrim took him beyond the sunset, and as heaven's morning broke, I like to think—in the words of Bunyan—that "all the trumpets sounded on the other side."

Former President George Bush spoke with tears in his eyes.

Reverend Billy Graham, who I refer to as the nation's pastor, is now hospitalized and regrets that he can't be here today. And I asked him for a Bible passage that might be appropriate. And he suggested this from Psalm 37: "The Lord delights in the way of the man whose steps he has made firm. Though he stumble, he will not fall, for the Lord upholds him with his hand."

Finally our President George W. Bush spoke with eloquence and grace about the strength of this humble man.

And where does that strength come from? Where is that courage learned? It is the faith of a boy who read the Bible with his mom. It is the faith of a man lying in an operating room who prayed for the one who shot him before he prayed for himself. It is the faith of a man with a fearful illness who waited on the Lord to call him home.

Now death has done all that death can do, and as Ronald Wilson Reagan goes his way, we are left with the joyful hope he shared. In his last years he saw through a glass darkly. Now he sees his Savior face to face.

Barry and I had calculated what time the casket would arrive back in California for burial. We didn't want to miss a moment of this evening's ceremony.

As eight o'clock approached here in Nashville, I should have been sitting in front of my television at home, but I was not. I was in the last place that I planned to be. Let me take you there.

## You Did What?

I was sitting in the emergency room at Baptist Hospital. It was busy and noisy. Two police officers brought in a belligerent drunk who had fallen and cut his face. They sat him beside me. He leaned against my shoulder and drooled on my shirt. Then he swayed forward and drooled on my computer. I moved. He followed me, offering to show me what was in his paper sack! I resisted the kind offer. Finally he screamed at the top of his voice, "This is it! Let it begin, then let it end!" And with that pronouncement out of his system, he fell off his chair.

I grabbed my computer, which had jumped into the air as he screamed. The receptionist rolled her eyes. His outburst didn't move her at all. A woman in a wheelchair was throwing up in a sack. I offered to help, but she looked at me with mistrust and hissed something about leaving her purse alone. The couple opposite me was arguing.

"I told you to stay off that ladder!"

"Well, if you had hung the picture when I asked you, I wouldn't have been up the ladder!"

Time passed. I looked at the screen of the waiting-room television and could see the convoy carrying the casket of President Reagan to his body's resting place move along the Southern California freeway. Crowds of people lined the side of the road, their cars pulled over in respect. Men, women, and children hung over every overpass and bridge. I saw a flag suspended over the freeway and wondered if Mrs. Reagan expected all of this.

The drunken man found his way back onto his feet and tracked me down. He swayed in front of me, cackling like a hyena. I hate emergency rooms! Finally they called my name. I hobbled through the door and pulled myself onto a bed in my assigned cubicle. My left ankle was swollen to twice its size; it was black and blue, and somewhere deep inside a throbbing pulse was playing the *1812 Overture* with great gusto. A young nurse assured me that someone would be there shortly. Having experienced "shortly" before, I lay back on the bed and wondered if I could call my husband on my cell phone. I decided against it and closed my eyes.

Sometime later the curtain that was around my cubicle was pulled back with dramatic flair, so I sat up.

"How did you do this?" a male nurse inquired.

I tried to think of more noble explanations than the pitiful truth: *A young mother lost control of her stroller. It was hurtling toward an oncoming vehicle, so I threw myself in its path and pushed the stroller to safety.* Or *I pulled a boy free from the mouth of a rabid wolf. It bit me, but it's a mere flesh wound.*

I looked in his tired eyes and knew that he had no patience left for baloney. I confessed, "I was taking my dog for a walk, and I fell off the sidewalk."

I find it amazing how, with no words, some people have the gift to communicate, *What an idiot.*

I was taken to have the offending limb x-rayed. "Does it hurt when I twist it like this?" the x-ray technician asked.

"Well—yes!" I said with tears in my eyes, feeling like a big baby.

Several x-rays later, I was wheeled back to my cubicle and told that the doctor would be in "shortly."

When the doctor had examined the x-rays, she came and sat on the edge of my bed. "So you fell off the sidewalk?" she asked with a twinkle in her eyes.

"It was a big sidewalk," I whispered sheepishly.

"Well, it's not broken, but you have done some damage. You've torn the ligaments in your ankle. We will fit you with a surgical boot, and you will need to use crutches for a while. I'll prescribe some pain medication for the first few days. It will make you sleepy and your thoughts a little cloudy, so don't write anything important, and don't climb any stairs."

I started to laugh. I laughed and laughed. She looked at me wondering, I'm sure, if she should transfer me across the street to the psychiatric unit. I thanked her, grabbed my crutches, and hobbled out. I couldn't explain my hysteria; it was too long a story. But those two simple pieces of advice couldn't have been more ridiculous to me at that time. I had a book due the following month, and we had just moved from our home into an apartment up three flights of stairs!

I called Barry, who was home with our seven-year-old son, Christian, and told him the good news that I hadn't broken my ankle. I decided to save the rest for later. I drove back to the apartment and parked my car and grabbed my crutches. I had no idea how difficult it is to use them for the first time. It's like that old patting your head and rubbing your tummy exercise; it looks easy but is frustratingly difficult. I made it across the parking lot and sat on the bottom step, looking at the three flights above me, and decided that I would just pitch a tent there at the bottom. I reflected on the past months' events.

"This is not the best time to write a book on faith, Lord," I said. "I don't know if You've noticed that?"

There was no immediate answer, but it started to rain.

## Events Cloud the Sky

It would be nice to think that one could write in a vacuum. I would find it easier if, when the day arrived to begin a manuscript, I could put life on hold until I was finished. Then I could simply write out of what *had* happened and reflect on those events as opposed to what is *continuing* to happen and interrupting my writing schedule with annoying frequency.

Four events have occurred during the last few months, demanding attention and time that I didn't have. But they have been loud and persistent. I think of them as

Grand larceny in San Jose;
An unexpected e-mail;
A devastating car crash;
The great uprooting.

All of these events seem unconnected, but I can't escape the conviction that they are strongly linked. I'll tell you why as we explore them in this chapter and those following. For that I'll need to go back in time and give you a brief history of an organization that I am part of—Women of Faith—for that commitment has led me to this theme and this book at this time.

## The Path to *Extraordinary Faith*

I am part of a team of six women who have traveled across America together since 1996, presenting conferences. These weekend events for women became a reality in January of that year. Our first year's theme was *A Joyful Journey* and conferences were held, and sold out, in ten U.S. cities, with a total attendance of thirty thousand women. Now we travel to thirty cities every year, and more than two million women have attended Women of Faith events since 1996. What started out as a simple idea has evolved into one of the most significant and powerful women's movements of this decade. It is very clear to us as a team that the idea came from the heart of God. Each of us considers it to be a great privilege to partner with God in communicating His overwhelming love to women in our nation and, through our writing, to the world. I had no idea as a young woman growing up in a small town on the west coast of Scotland that God would give me such an amazing gift.

As our tenth anniversary approached, we discussed what our theme should be for 2005. The majority felt compelled by the topic of *Extraordinary Faith.* I didn't initially warm to this idea. I love talking about the love of God, about His grace and compassion, but I am a little intimidated by faith. Perhaps my reluctance is a residue of the so-called faith movement of the 1980s.

At that time I was the cohost of *The 700 Club* with Dr. Pat Robertson. Pat is a man who believes in the healing power of God, in praying for the sick and expecting miracles. Having worked with him for five years, I have tremendous respect for him, but at times we differed in our understanding of God's ways. I believe with all my heart that God can heal, but it seems to me that in these days, this is the exception rather than the rule. I have lost many friends to cancer; I have stood with others as they have buried their children even though they were godly people who had asked God to spare their loved ones.

The issue that troubles me most with faith is the burden many carry when they don't get the answers they have prayed for; they feel they have failed in some way. That seems a cruel yoke to wear in the midst of pain. I have received their letters and heard their pain-filled words.

"If I had more faith, my child would not have died."
"If I had more faith, I would find a husband."

"If I had more faith, this curse of cancer would leave me."

"If I had more faith . . ."

"If I had more faith . . ."

(Now, the irony that I am part of a team called Women of Faith has not escaped me!)

During my tenure as cohost of *The 700 Club,* we aired stories of those who had experienced God's miraculous intervention in their lives. The stories were inspiring and, Pat believes, faith-building. My problem was that when all you show are the stories with the happy endings, it can seem to those watching that God always responds that way if you have enough faith. Therefore, if your child dies or your husband doesn't come home, you have failed in some way.

Pat does not believe that, but I received thousands of letters from those who gleaned that message as they compared what we aired to the reality of their own lives. My heart ached for God's people who were longing to find some mysterious key that would unlock the answers they desired.

I am aware of the Scriptures that proclaim the impact of simple faith, and during this journey together we will study those texts, but in this opening discourse I just wanted to come clean with you as to where I am as we begin.

So we chose the theme for 2005 even as I squirmed slightly under the weight of the title. To add irony to irony, our Women of Faith president, Mary Graham, who is one of my dearest friends on this earth, asked me if I would like to write the theme book for the year.

"I can't write on faith, Mary. I don't have enough. Sometimes when I pray for people, they get worse. I'm kind of like Lourdes in reverse!"

"I don't think that's the point," she said. "I don't think it's about us. I think it's all about God."

So I said that I would and was grateful for the opportunity to examine an area that is troubling to me. I had no idea that I was then walking toward the first of four apparently unconnected events.

## Grand Larceny in San Jose

I opened my eyes to a beautiful, sunny California morning. Barry, Christian, and I had flown in from our home in Nashville the night before. We were in San Jose for one of our 2004 conferences. Our theme for that year was *Irrepressible Hope.*

The conferences begin on Friday night and go through Saturday. Our family's usual schedule was to fly in on Thursday nights during the school year so that Christian missed only one day a week of first grade. His school administration was very understanding and supportive of the work that God has called me to, and his teacher sent his Friday work on the road with us.

That weekend was going to be a little different, though. (I just had no idea at the time how different it would prove to be.) We had flown in on Wednesday evening, as we had been invited to join Mary Graham and Luci Swindoll, one of my fellow speakers, on a tour of Mrs. Grossman's Sticker Factory, the oldest and largest sticker company in the USA. Andrea Grossman is quite a powerhouse. She began her sticker venture in 1979 as a small home business, working from her dining-room table. Now she has 160 employees and prints more than fifteen thousand miles of stickers a year—enough to go halfway around the globe! Luci had been there before and raved about the tour, but to be honest, I was less than excited.

"Stickers? We're going to spend a whole day looking at stickers?" I asked Barry when he told me about the invitation.

"I think Christian will love it," he said.

"I'm sure he will. He's seven. I'm forty-seven. A whole day, a whole long day looking at stickers when I need to work?" I questioned.

"It will be good for you," Barry continued. "You need a break. How much of your book have you written?"

"About a third," I said. "I have a long way to go."

Barry gave me one of those persuasive looks that I have always found irresistible. So we bundled into a van on Thursday morning and headed north along the lovely coastline of Northern California. As the

Golden Gate Bridge gleamed ahead of us, I asked Luci how far we still had to go.

"It's about a two-hour trip," she said.

"Two hours! Two hours! Barry, you said it was forty minutes."

"I said 'roughly forty minutes,'" he replied sheepishly.

Christian laughed out loud, so I parked my indignation and decided to lighten up. In no time at all (!!) we were there. I have to tell you, it is an amazing place. I am not a sticker woman—or at least I didn't used to be—but Mrs. Grossman can find the latent sticker soul inside us all.

The facility itself is very impressive. They currently manufacture more than seven hundred different stickers and add new designs all the time. Their presses run twenty-four hours a day, five days a week. The plant is located on a protected wildlife preserve brimming with birds of all kinds, and since the walls are all made of glass, it is a nature lover's paradise. Tours take about one hour. We started with an award-winning twenty-minute video narrated by the company mascot, Angus, an Australian shepherd.

Mrs. Grossman has a policy that if you have a well-behaved dog, you should bring it to work with you. Christian was lost in doggy heaven. He fell in love with a tiny Pomeranian and tried to make a deal with its owner. "I will give you everything I own if I can have Tina!"

Tina's "mom" resisted.

Christian spent a large part of the day lying on the floor, hugging the other large hairy beasts. Then we toured the factory and took a card-making class. I loved it. Soon it was time to head back to our hotel with armloads of free stickers. The drive back was pretty; the sun was beginning to set over San Francisco. We stopped at In-and-Out Burgers. Barry told Christian that the restaurant was owned by a believer and that the biblical reference John 3:16 was on the bottom of every soda cup. I just wish he had waited until Christian had finished his drink before he passed on that interesting piece of information!

When we got back to our room, I sat down at the desk to get to work while Barry checked out the room service menu. (Apparently the two burgers, waffle fries, and a pie were now a distant memory!)

I sat and stared at the desk. I closed my eyes and opened them and stared some more. I got up and walked around the room, then sat down again. "I need new glasses," I said.

"I thought you just got those," Barry replied.

"I did, but they're not working."

"What do you mean, 'not working'?" he asked.

"Well, I can't see my computer."

"Where is it?" he asked.

"On this desk," I replied.

"No, it's not," he said.

"Yes, it is. I left it there this morning."

"Well, it's not there now. You must have moved it," he suggested.

"I didn't. I remember exactly where I left it because I checked my e-mail right before we left."

I sat for a few moments avoiding reality, but then I knew. I knew that someone had broken into our room and stolen my computer. In that same moment I realized with sickening reality that I had not backed up one word of my book. I always do. I either burn it to a CD or send it to my assistant or editor, but I had been so busy and so pressured that I had forgotten to do that.

We called hotel security and, as the evening progressed it became clear from the maid who had cleaned our room that morning that when she came to our door it was wide open. She had reported it but had no way of knowing if anything was missing.

"Did you save your work?" Barry whispered.

"No," I said as a big tired tear slipped down my cheek.

Christian was very upset. "Mom, I will sell all my toys and buy you a new one," he said with typical compassion.

I realized that this was one of those moments when my son was watching to see how to respond when life takes an unexpected turn. We sat on the bed together. "Thank you, sweet pea. That is so kind of you, but you don't have to do that. We have a great opportunity here. Either we believe that God is good and He is in control of everything that happens in our lives, or we don't. I believe that He is. I believe it with all my heart."

"Then why didn't He stop the person taking your computer?" he asked, his big brown eyes full of questions.

"I don't know, darling," I said. "We don't always understand what happens, but if we believe God, and if we trust Him, we can be sure that He is watching over us."

"Well, I think it stinks, Mom," he said, his eyes brimming over with tears.

"Me, too, and the great thing is that we get to feel our feelings. But underneath all that, we are offered peace because God is good, not just some of the time but all the time."

I pulled out my Bible and I read those famous words from Paul's letter to the Romans: "And we know that all things work together for good to those who love God, to those who are the called according to His purpose. For whom He foreknew, He also predestined to be conformed to the image of His Son" (Rom. 8:28–29 NKJV).

"What does that mean, Mom?" he asked.

"It means that even when bad things happen, God will bring good out of them, because that's who He is. The whole point of this life is that we become like Jesus," I told Christian. Then I joked, "Perhaps God didn't like what I wrote so far, so He had someone take it so I could start again!"

My son is a very literal child. He spent much of the next day telling people that God got someone to take my computer because what I had written so far "stunk"!

So I was back to square one and word one. I offered a reward if anyone would return my computer or even download my work onto a disk or CD and keep the computer, but to no avail.

I had prayed a lot about writing this book and was sure that God had called me to do it; I simply hadn't anticipated how difficult the beginning would be. I talked with my friend and fellow Woman of Faith speaker Marilyn Meberg about my frustration.

"It seems crazy," I said. "Here I am writing a book on faith, and if the circumstances around me are anything to go by, then I am coming up very short!"

She reminded me of our theme verse for 2005, "Now faith is the substance of things hoped for, the evidence of things not seen" (Heb. 11:1 NKJV).

"Well, I had hoped to finish this book in my lifetime," I said, "but the evidence certainly doesn't support that."

She laughed and said, "That might be the whole point. We don't need faith for things we can see clearly. We need faith when the path ahead is dark."

## "I'M DOING THIS FOR GOD!"

I received a letter from a young woman in her twenties who believed that God had called her to be a missionary in Africa. Her note was overflowing with frustration and confusion.

In her mind she believed that she was holding up her end of the deal, leaving family and friends and everything that was familiar and comfortable to her to respond to God's leading, so why was it so difficult? She went on to list a myriad of little details that hadn't fallen into place when she expected them to. I understood her frustration and her thinking process. She felt that if she was stepping out in faith, then God would make the path straight. That's not always so. I've heard her disappointment echoed many times.

"I volunteered to lead the women's Bible study, but no one appreciates what I'm doing."

"I'm trying to get my husband saved, but everything I do seems to push him farther away!"

"I've been faithful in raising my children in the church, so why is God allowing them to turn away now?"

If you are like me, you want life to be more black and white than grey. I like things to make sense to me. I want to be able to understand what God is doing, but that's not always the case. Sometimes the plans we have made, the hopes and dreams we carry, fall apart at our feet. Are you in that place now? Do you wonder if God has abandoned you, or if you have missed God somewhere along the path?

It is the loneliest place on earth as a believer to feel as if God has left you or to live with the taunting voice that says you have blown it and missed God's best for your life. As we walk through this book together, I pray that we will receive a clearer picture of what it means to walk by faith, no matter what sight tells us.

Perhaps that is the whole point of faith: that we follow God faithfully when nothing makes sense anymore. As Eugene Peterson wrote, we are called to walk *A Long Obedience in the Same Direction.*

As a family, we were about to face some changes in our lives, as were some of my friends. These events made me take a much deeper look at faith than I had ever done. Through two catastrophic events one friend seemed to have every prayer answered even more than we could ask for, and for the other it was as if there were cracks in the floor of the throne room of grace and all our words fell back to earth unheard. Perhaps you have been there? Let's read on.

# CHAPTER 2

# THE BEST OF TIMES AND THE WORST OF TIMES

## *When We Receive the Answer We Prayed for— or the Answer We Dreaded*

∽

*To God I cried with mournful voice,*
*I sought His gracious ear,*
*In the sad day when troubles rose,*
*And filled the night with fear.*
*Sad were my days, and dark my nights,*
*My soul refused relief;*
*I thought on God the just and wise,*
*But thoughts increased my grief.*

—Isaac Watts


*I will bring the blind by a way they did not know;*
*I will lead them in paths they have not known.*
*I will make darkness light before them,*
*And crooked places straight.*
*These things I will do for them,*
*And not forsake them.*

—Isaiah 42:16 NKJV


Nashville is a city brimming with those involved in Christian ministry. We have a large community of wonderful musicians, singers, and songwriters, which is quite a siren call for many aspiring artists who hope to be "discovered" if they move here. A young girl wrote to me and said that she was going to move to Nashville just so she could hang with all the artists whose CDs she played in her car every day. "It will be a little foretaste of heaven," she wrote.

I wrote back and told her that it wasn't quite like that. It's unlikely that you would walk into McDonald's and see Michael W. Smith, CeCe Winans, Randy Travis, and Point of Grace in the play area.

Even though I have many friends involved in ministry who live here in town, we have to make a concerted effort to get together because we all travel so much. It seems that e-mails these days have become the equivalent of leaning over the fence and chatting with friends and neighbors.

E-mail would never be my first choice. I am a face-to-face person. I don't even really like the phone. I like to sit with my friends and look in their eyes, for I think that eyes speak as loudly as words.

I have fond memories of different days when I was growing up and the pace of life was much slower; it seemed kinder and more conducive to community. But for the moment, this is the place God has me in, so every year I look forward to the months of December, January, and February. During those three months we have no conferences. I treasure that time. These are days rich with shared meals, having friends over for a relaxed cup of coffee, and usually a trip to Scotland to be with my family. I think of it as my big catch-up and refueling of the year.

## AN UNEXPECTED E-MAIL

On the morning of January 2, 2004, I signed on to the Internet and checked my e-mail. I deleted several unsolicited messages from sources telling me they could help me shed those extra Christmas pounds in record time and scanned for familiar names. I saw that I had a message from my friend, Janice Chaffee. Janice has a heart for women. She and her husband, Jim, have worked in the Christian music world for a long time. It became apparent to Janice that behind the smiles and the success of many women in the industry were shame and fear. She began to write to that need. Her first book, *Sisters: The Story Goes On,* was a call to honesty, integrity, and community. Her latest work, *If the Prodigal Were a Daughter,* is a retelling of four of Jesus' parables, this time with a largely female cast, which gives fresh light and meaning for contemporary women. (Visit www.janicechaffee.com for more information and updates on Janice.)

I clicked on Janice's message, thinking that it had been some time since we had seen each other. From the first line I knew that something was seriously wrong. She wrote:

Dear Family and Friends,

I wanted you to hear directly from me how my life drastically changed in just twelve hours last Monday. But, first, a little background information.

A couple of weeks ago, I got new eyeglasses. The right lens didn't seem "right" but the technician said to take time to get used to the new prescription. So I squinted and bobbed my head up and down, trying to find focus, to the point that my eyeball felt like it was going to explode. A few days before Christmas, my right eyelid became inflamed, swollen, red and heavy. I had just finished up some antibiotics for a sinus infection so I thought the infection had settled there or that I had a cold in my eye. Then on Christmas night, slathering anti-wrinkle cream around my eyes, I felt a small numb spot on my right temple. That's odd, I thought to myself. By Sunday, Dec. 28, my entire temple was numb, from my eyebrow down to my cheekbone.

So the next morning I called my GP and was given a 1:45 appointment. I told the entire story; can't see clearly out of my right eye, swollen lid, numbness in the temple. All I wanted was a prescription. I was told to get an MRI. I resisted. After a brief battle of wills, the doctor went to the lobby and asked Jim to come into the room. The doctor handed him a prescription for a steroid pack (to reduce swelling) along with an order for an MRI at the local hospital, just to "make sure there's no bad stuff causing the swelling of the nerves," the doctor said. "It could be Bells Palsy, which basically heals by itself, or it could be MS. We want to rule out any bad things." The order had STAT written on it in big, black letters (should have been a clue). The doctor told Jim to drive me straight to outpatient; the staff was waiting for me.

When the MRI was over, Jim and I asked the technician, "So, what do we do now?" He told us to go home and wait for the doctor's phone call. Jim cooked a great meal, served our plates, and as we walked toward the television, the phone rang. I answered to hear my doctor say, "I'm afraid I have some bad news. You have a tumor behind your right eye."

The doctor instructed me to be at the hospital on Wednesday morning, Dec. 31, at 7:00 for a bone marrow aspiration and biopsy.

The doctor was truthful: the first shot did feel like a bee sting; the second burned, and, yes, the only true pain was when he sucked out the marrow. After five seconds of excruciating torture, he stopped and so did the pain. I was given a good blast of Demerol and slept like a baby.

I must insert here that the presence of God has been around me—and the care of the nurses, especially Johnny, who attended to me all day with tender compassion. She prayed for me and promised, as she wheeled me to the exit, that God would be faithful.

My moment of truth will come this afternoon, Jan. 2, 2004, at 1:15. An oncologist will have reviewed all the blood samples, the bone marrow, the MRI, the CT scans and x-rays and will, hopefully, give us a proper diagnosis. I've been prepared that I may have a dose of radiation to stop the tumor's growth.

So, I will stop writing now; it's a little after 10:00 on Friday. I am bruised, sore, aching, and afraid. I will finish this later today, after I've heard the news. Whatever it is, God is in control. Good or bad, I know that the Christ Child, named Emmanuel, is the promise of God With Us. Even in this nightmare that won't let me wake up, I know that.

I love you dearly and ask that you keep me in your prayers. Please be just as fervent for Jim and Elliott and Taylor.

I'll write later—trusting in the peace that passes understanding.


Janice


I was stunned. I had rushed through the e-mail when I sensed that horrible, sickening, *knowing* in the pit of my stomach that life had just taken a sharp left turn for my friend. I wanted to get to the bit where she would say, "But praise God, they discovered that it was nothing, just an infection, just a false alarm, one of those moments that makes you stop, take a breath, and appreciate your life afresh." I searched and searched, but it wasn't there.

In a follow-up note, Janice asked those she shared her story with not to call the house for a few days, as life was very up in the air for the whole family. E-mails, though, were welcome. I wrote back. I didn't know what to say, but I have learned over the last few years that there is no right thing to say; I should just be there.

When my mother-in-law, Eleanor, was diagnosed with liver cancer, I watched as some friends moved in closer and some distanced themselves. I understood the distance. Our mortality is a hard reality to face. Cancer has become such a dividing line through our families and culture. We seem to hear about more and more of it every day and not just with those who have made poor life choices, but ordinary, healthy men and women. Their lives and struggles can seem like a mirror to those who live in fear of such a diagnosis. I watched as many of Eleanor's friends were reluctant to look in her eyes, afraid of what might be reflected there.

All that I knew to say to Janice was that I loved her and would be praying for and with her every step of the way.

## Suffering Multiplied

Her next update two days later brought very bad news. Her doctor confirmed that she has multiple myeloma. She wrote, "It is evident not only behind my right eye, but also in my left humerus (arm), two places in my left femur (thigh), one place on my right femur, one shoulder (I think left) and some of my ribs."

I went online and searched every site that might have relevant information about this type of cancer. The typical prognosis is not good, but then Janice is not typical, and when God is involved anything can happen. A couple of weeks later a mutual friend, Sue Buchanan, wrote to me and said that Janice wanted to have a party just to be with as many of her girlfriends in one room at the same time as she could. Sue asked if I could host it at my house. I checked the date and saw that I would be in South Bend, Indiana that day for a television interview but could be back late in the afternoon. I talked to Barry, and he said he would be glad to do as much preparation as I needed. Christian said that he wanted to help too.

We decided that he would be the official coat-taker. (On a side note, at the end of the party we still had two coats left over that no one has ever claimed. I'm not sure if Christian in his fervor to help suggested that coats could be donated to Janice!)

It was a very special evening. Janice wrote of her memories of the night.

February 10th was a great day. After getting fitted with a sassy, saucy wig, my friend Barb and I returned home and dressed for a party—a party for ME! Sue Buchanan hosted a fabulous bash at Sheila Walsh's home. About 60 of my local friends showed up to celebrate life and all that life brings—including cancer.

Everyone moved among tables laden with food, chatting and munching, meeting each other (my friends know no strangers!), finding connections. Then, finally, we were all herded into one room where we shared the greatest of laughs and the deepest of tears.

And did we laugh! And, yes, we did cry. When asked questions about my diagnosis and future recovery—then the tears flowed. Even though the medical reports are not that promising (only a 3–5 year remission after a stem cell replacement), I believe that God is the Great Healer and that my future is in God's hands. The party was fun and evidence of the power of friendship. I am a blessed woman; absolutely every person should be in the center of attention at least once in their lives, to feel loved and cared for by so many.

## THE BATTLE CONTINUES

As I write, Janice continues to battle with this disease and the side effects of the drugs she is taking. She has a large community of friends and family who love her and are committed to walk with her through the ups and downs of the journey. One thing that has become apparent to us all, however, is that there are few ups. Everything that could go wrong has gone wrong. She is surrounded by faithful prayer warriors and a community of women friends who go with her to every hospital appointment, but nothing has gone right.

Treatments have had to be cancelled due to infections, veins have refused to accept the chemo that brings hope in a poisonous cocktail, her face is numb and her body bruised and battered. The list is endless: clogged port-a-catheter, blood clots, infections, pneumonia, allergic reaction to antibiotics, removal of the first PICC line, skin rash from thalidomide, hallucinations from sleeping pills, swelling from steroids, the most recent bruises from vasculitis, and the resurgence of cancer during the week she was off all meds.

I find myself saying over and over, "When will she get a break?" Many times I read her e-mails with tears rolling down my face. I don't understand this path that she has been diverted onto. I know that God loves her with great passion and tenderness. I know, too, that He is able to heal her completely right now without the barbaric treatment that He graces her to submit herself to, but as of this moment He has not.

What seems cruel and unusual to me, though, is that she has to fight far more than the cancer. As she heads toward her stem-cell replacement, she encounters one road block after another. Last night I sent her the lyrics to one of my favorite hymns written by Fanny Crosby.

> Jesus, keep me near the cross,
> There a precious fountain
> Free to all—a healing stream
> Flows from Calvary's mountain.
> In the cross, in the cross,
> Be my glory ever;
> Till my raptured soul shall find
> Rest beyond the river.
>
> Near the cross, a trembling soul,
> Love and mercy found me;
> There the Bright and Morning Star
> Sheds its beams around me.
>
> Near the cross! O Lamb of God,
> Bring its scenes before me;
> Help me walk from day to day,
> With its shadows o'er me.

Today before I began to write, I checked for messages and Janice had replied.

Thank you for the lyric to "Near the Cross." I've printed it out and will carry it with me, especially today. Already this morning, disaster. My right eyelid (top and bottom) is infected and nearly swollen shut. One more thing gone wrong, one more prescription to take with all the other drugs. The "other" problems combined with the cancer make this battle seem almost insurmountable. Almost. Days like today are deflating and disappointing, but wonderfully counterbalanced by the hope of friends, the comfort of old hymns, the promises of Scripture. Thank you for reminding me to stay near the cross. I shall rest there today, in its shadow.

—Janice

I am humbled by the faith of my friend. I am humbled by her vulnerability. I am humbled by her honest expression of grief and struggle and fear and yet the clear song of faith that she sings through it all. It's a different song from what I once imagined. It's not a song that tells us that if we just have enough faith, everything in our lives will be smooth and easy. At times this new song is in a minor key, and the notes seem lonely and bleak; but the song of faith is one that tells all that is true within the context of the greatness of God.

## AN ANGUISHED KING SINGS A FAITH-FILLED SONG

David knew how to sing the song of faith. He and Janice seem to sing together these days.

> My soul is in anguish.
> > How long, O LORD, how long?
> Turn, O LORD, and deliver me;
> > save me because of your unfailing love.
> . . . I am worn out from groaning;
> > all night long I flood my bed with weeping
> > and drench my couch with tears.
> . . . Away from me, all you who do evil,
> > for the LORD has heard my weeping.
> The LORD has heard my cry for mercy;
> the LORD accepts my prayer.

—Psalm 6:3–4, 6, 8–9

How long must I wrestle with my thoughts
    and every day have sorrow in my heart?
. . . But I trust in your unfailing love;
    my heart rejoices in your salvation.
I will sing to the LORD,
    for he has been good to me.

—Psalm 13:2, 5–6

Within the same song David cried out what was true and harsh, and yet he reaffirmed his faith in God, who heard him and loved him. At times theologians have struggled with David's brutal honesty. Some prayer books have performed *psalmectomies*—edited out the most raw emotion as if protecting us. That seems wrong to me unless they can also protect us from the realities of life. We need the companionship of other honest souls who have wrestled with their faith and said out loud what is rumbling around in their souls.

I remember a conversation I had with a woman at a conference in Chicago. I had spoken that night about my struggle with depression, my stay in a psychiatric hospital, and my ongoing use of medication. She was in my book line, and I didn't see her face until she was right in front of me. I have an absolute commitment that I look only at the woman I am with at that moment. The arenas are teeming with thousands of women, but I block them all out so that I can listen to whatever the next woman has to say.

I looked up in her eyes, and I could tell the pain that she was in. Her eyes filled with tears that ran like rivers down her face. It took her a few moments to be able to speak. When she did, it was in broken sentences as she gasped for air. "You stood up there . . . you told my story . . . you said it out loud. I can't . . . I can't believe it."

I understood exactly what she meant. So often we are afraid to say what is true because we are ashamed. We feel that if we say it out loud, we will self-combust.

Janice has given those of us who know and love her the gift of saying out loud what is in our hearts, the raw pain and the real faith. Many of you are there too. You have shared your stories with me in letters or in person and your faith has touched my life deeply. I am grateful for you and amazed. I think again today of Mary Graham's words to me—"faith is not about us, it's about God's gift to us when we need it most."

As the next event entered my life, it became clear to me that not only is life unpredictable, but so, too, are the ways of God. He is always good, but His goodness manifests itself in many different ways.

## A Devastating Car Crash

In March 2004, Women of Faith held its first national conference. We invited women from all across the country to join us in San Antonio, Texas, for a one-of-a-kind event. It was truly amazing to look at those gathered in the Alamo Dome; they represented all fifty states. (Technically only forty-nine, but since one woman had a beach house in the remaining state, we counted that!) All the musicians who had been our guests over the years were present, and we also welcomed some new faces to our stage.

It was a three-day event. The conference began on Thursday night. Sandi Patty was a guest musician, and Max Lucado was our special guest speaker on Friday night and Saturday morning. Cindy Cruse-Ratcliff joined our worship team and brought a sixty-voice choir from Lakewood Church in Houston. The comedienne Chonda Pierce spoke that night. She is one of the funniest people on the planet, and our audience loved her. I spoke after Chonda, and then Kathy Troccoli brought Sandi Patty, Babbie Mason, Point of Grace, Natalie Grant, Nicole Nordeman, Patti Cabrera, and Tammy Trent onstage for a final song. Patsy Clairmont and Thelma Wells spoke on Friday morning, and Marilyn Meberg in the afternoon. At three o'clock the arena was cleared to get ready for a concert that night. It was quite an experience to be there.

When the concert was over, Max Lucado brought a brief devotion to direct our hearts to worshiping God, the Giver of all life and light. That led into our worship event, which was one of the most moving experiences of my life. The Alamo Dome was filled with thousands of voices lifted in praise to God. On Saturday morning Max brought his main message. He spoke eloquently and tenderly on Psalm 23.

> The LORD is my shepherd;
> I shall not want.
> He makes me to lie down in green pastures;
> He leads me beside the still waters.
> He restores my soul;
> He leads me in the paths of righteousness
> For His name's sake.
> Yea, though I walk through the valley of the shadow of death,
> I will fear no evil;
> For You are with me;
> Your rod and Your staff, they comfort me.
> You prepare a table before me in the presence of my enemies;
> You anoint my head with oil;
> My cup runs over.
> Surely goodness and mercy shall follow me
> All the days of my life;
> And I will dwell in the house of the LORD
> Forever. (NKJV)

It was a powerful reminder to each one of us that we have a personal Shepherd watching over us at all times. My friends, Chris and Jan Harris, were with us in San Antonio. Chris has produced my last two CD projects, so I was thrilled that he was able to hear performed live what we had worked on in the studio. They had no idea as they listened to Max's message how much they would need it in just a few hours—but God did.

I had just walked back into our house that Sunday when the phone rang. It was Mary Graham telling us that as we were in the Alamo Dome together, Chris and Jan's son, Brandon, had been in a terrible car crash. She didn't know if he was going to make it or not. I was horrified. Brandon was a student at the same school Christian attended and was about to graduate high school.

I called Chris. He was with Jan at Vanderbilt Hospital's intensive care unit. He told me that the crash had been horrific. Brandon had many fractures and rips in his heart and in his liver. He asked for prayer. That night I sent out an emergency request for Brandon to those who receive my weekly newsletter, about thirty-five thousand people. By the next morning I couldn't believe the responses. They poured in from coast to coast across America, from Scotland, Australia, Germany, England, and South Africa. My assistant, Martie, printed out as many as she could, and I took them to Chris and Jan that night in the intensive care waiting room. It meant the world to them to know that brothers and sisters they have never met were upholding their son.

It is a miracle that Brandon survived this terrible crash. He had so many fractures—but one of the most severe injuries was a testimony of God's grace. Jan told me that the worst fracture, a broken femur, actually saved Brandon's life. It pierced the skin, put him into shock and lowered his blood pressure, ensuring that the heart did not pump out too much blood through the tear. Even in disaster God's hand was so apparent.

When Christian and I arrived at the hospital (Barry was in Dallas), I was very moved by the number of Brandon's school friends who were there. Christian recognized a few of the senior boys. He asked me over and over as he spotted a face he knew, "Why is he here?" I told him the same thing each time, "Because he loves God and he loves Brandon and wants to be there for him." Christian said, "There's a lot of love here."

At every step in Brandon's road to recovery, God's grace and favor have been apparent. He has beaten every deadline in terms of recovery. After a few days he was moved to Vanderbilt's rehabilitation unit. I decided to take another batch of encouraging e-mails along on a visit. I didn't expect to see him because I knew he was in intense therapy. The receptionist was warm and kind. As we talked it became apparent that she was a believer.

"There are a lot of people praying for this boy," she said.

"I know. Isn't it awesome?" I replied. "That why I'm here. These are notes and promises of prayer from people all around the world." I held up a thick wad of paper.

She directed me to the floor where Brandon's new room was located. Compared to the buzz of the ICU waiting room, everything was quiet, and I stooped down to push the papers under the door just as Jan appeared. She told me that Brandon was in his room, and I could go in if I wanted to. I asked if she would check with him to see if he felt up to it. "Not every teenage boy wants someone the age of his mother hanging out," I said.

Brandon was gracious enough to welcome me in. As I hugged him, I was overwhelmed at the miracle before me. He is such a sweet boy, a talented guitarist with a very dry sense of humor that I love. Just like a boy, he asked me if I wanted to see his wounds! We chatted for a while, and I gave him the pile of e-mails. His eyes filled with tears as he read the first few. "This is cool!" he said.

He had many challenges in the days and weeks ahead. There was weakness on the right side of his body (related to the head injury on the left side of his head). There was still swelling from the head injury. He had surgery on his left leg to attempt to get all the bones to fuse together properly. His wrist was broken on his guitar-strumming hand, and I have a feeling that he might have directed all of his prayers in that direction!

But in stark contrast to Janice, everything with Brandon went better than anyone could have expected. He was even able to attend his high school prom in a wheelchair.

Here we have two believers who live just a few miles away from each other in Nashville, Tennessee, both crying out to the same God for mercy and healing, both being carried in the arms of those who love them. It reminded me of the story found in Luke 5.

One day as he was teaching, Pharisees and teachers of the law, who had come from every village of Galilee and from Judea and Jerusalem, were sitting there. And the power of the Lord was present for him to heal the sick. Some men came carrying a paralytic on a mat and tried to take him into the house to lay him before Jesus. When they could not find a way to do this because of the crowd, they went up on the roof and lowered him on his mat through the tiles into the middle of the crowd, right in front of Jesus.

When Jesus saw their faith, he said, "Friend, your sins are forgiven." (vv. 17–20)

This is a beautiful picture of the body of Christ in action, carrying those who cannot carry themselves. Here is what I struggle with as I watch my friends: one is experiencing overwhelming mercy and relief, and the other is experiencing sustaining grace accompanied by increasing pain and struggle. Some days when I open my e-mail, there are notes about both of my friends. I read one and then the other, and the contrast is severe. It is clear that some of us receive the answers we hope for and some the answers we dread.

## Is God More Faithful in One Situation Than the Other?

I think of Rick Husband and the rest of the crew on the space shuttle *Columbia,* which burned up on its reentry into earth's atmosphere. The last time Evelyn, Rick's wife, saw him on the night before liftoff, he led a brief devotional for the crew and spouses and recited Joshua 1:5–9 from memory.

No one will be able to stand up against you all the days of your life. As I was with Moses, so I will be with you; I will never leave you nor forsake you. Be strong and courageous, because you will lead these people to inherit the land I swore to their forefathers to give them. Be strong and very courageous. Be careful to obey all the law my servant Moses gave you; do not turn from it to the right or to the left, that you may be successful wherever you go. Do not let this Book of the Law depart from your mouth; meditate on it day and night, so that you may be careful to do everything written in it. Then you will be prosperous and successful. Have I not commanded you? Be strong and courageous. Do not

be terrified; do not be discouraged, for the LORD your God will
be with you wherever you go.

This passage contains one of the most profound promises that God
has made to an individual human being. No one was more acquainted
with God's special relationship with Moses than Joshua. He was permit-
ted inside the Tent of Meeting and witnessed the face-to-face meetings of
Moses and the Lord. Joshua was intimately acquainted with the unique
relationship between Moses and God. Moses was the one who had
changed Joshua's name from Hoshea. *Joshua* means "the Lord delivers."

"No one will be able to stand up against you all the days of your
life. As I was with Moses, so I will be with you; I will never leave you
nor forsake you." This promise seems to indicate that whatever Joshua
decreed in his position of leadership, it would be accomplished just as
it was with Moses. Yet we know from Scripture that Moses encountered great rebellion among the people. When Joshua died, he was 110
years old. He had seen the fulfillment of much of what God had promised, but vast areas of land that the Israelites had been promised yet
remained in enemy hands. So what was God promising here to Joshua,
and does that promise extend to Rick Husband and his crew, to Janice,
to Brandon, and to you and me?

God gave some promises in Scripture to specific people in specific
situations, but the writer to the Hebrews echoed the promise to Joshua,
extending it to us: "God has said, 'Never will I leave you; never will I
forsake you.' So we say with confidence, 'The Lord is my helper; I will
not be afraid. What can man do to me?'" (13:5–6).

As with Moses, God says to you *I will be with you.*

The Lord God will be with you *wherever you go.*

As a young believer I wanted to think that if God was with me, He
would protect me from the harsher experiences in life, but that is not
the promise here. The promise is that wherever the path takes us, God
will be there. On that fateful morning, Evelyn Husband waited with
her daughter, Laura, and son, Matthew, and watched the clock on the
tarmac count down to the shuttle's return. She had no way of knowing

that when the clock said Rick would touch down in five minutes, he was already with Jesus.

Did God's words to Joshua, which Rick shared with his crew, fail?

Did they place their faith in a promise given to another man in a different time?

Evelyn says no! As the families were quickly taken off the tarmac into a private room, and it became clear that something had gone drastically wrong, Laura whispered to her mom, "God will get us through this."

Wherever Brandon is, God is with him.

Wherever Janice is, God is with her.

Whatever the Husband family is facing, God is with them.

Whatever you are facing right now, God is with you.

I find it significant that the words to that dear old hymn that brought comfort to my friend as she faced another mountain came from one who had been there too. Fanny Crosby would have loved to hold Janice, I am sure. She understood dark places.

Fanny Crosby was probably the most prolific hymnist in history. She was blinded by an incompetent doctor when she was only six weeks of age but went on to write more than eight thousand hymns. About her blindness, she said: "It seemed intended by the blessed providence of God that I should be blind all my life, and I thank him for the dispensation. If perfect earthly sight were offered me tomorrow I would not accept it. I might not have sung hymns to the praise of God if I had been distracted by the beautiful and interesting things about me." (See "The Cyber Hymnal" at http://www.cyberhymnal.org for more information on Fanny Crosby and her hymns.)

When she died, her tombstone carried the words "Blessed assurance, Jesus is mine! Oh, what a foretaste of glory divine!"

She had no way of knowing how the words she wrote, when her world was dark but her spirit full of light, would reach through the years and give my friend a shoulder to lean on when she needed it most. She had no way of knowing how her faith and faithfulness would impact others. Our lives send out ripples that affect so many people for good or evil.

## SPECIAL SIGHT

The waves of Fanny's love and faith touched another hymn writer whose songs I have sung since I was a child. When I was growing up, one of my mom's favorite records was of Burl Ives singing old hymns. I loved them all but would join in when he sang,

> Will there be any stars, any stars in my crown
> When at evening the sun goeth down?
> When I wake with the blest in the mansions of rest
> Will there be any stars in my crown?

I find it captivating how interwoven our lives as believers are. I have since discovered that lyric was written by Eliza Hewitt, who was moved deeply by Fanny Crosby's life and memorialized her passing in a lovely poem:

> Away to the country of sunshine and song,
> Our songbird has taken her flight,
> And she who has sung in the darkness so long
> Now sings in the beautiful light.

Believers' lives are wonderfully woven together in some tapestry greater than we can see at the moment. Fanny's words of faith touched Eliza, and she wrote a hymn that has become part of the fabric of my faith—just as Fanny's words are now bringing strength and faith to Janice.

As spring arrived in Tennessee in 2004, I knew that I had to get busy and start my book. Brandon's story was very present in my heart and mind, as was Janice's struggle. I just needed peace and quiet to work.

It was not to be. Enter Event #4.

# CHAPTER 3

# A Family Story

## *When God Says Go!*

⤳

*I'm but a stranger here, Heav'n is my home;*
*Earth is a desert drear, Heav'n is my home.*
*Danger and sorrow stand round me on every hand;*
*Heav'n is my fatherland, Heav'n is my home.*
—Thomas R. Taylor

*Do not lay up for yourselves treasures on earth, where*
*moth and rust destroy and where thieves break in and*
*steal; but lay up for yourselves treasures in heaven,*
*where neither moth nor rust destroys and where*
*thieves do not break in and steal. For where your*
*treasure is, there your heart will be also.*
—Matthew 6:19–21 NKJV

"Well, the pink bathroom will have to go," she said. "No man is going to want a house with a pink bathroom."

I looked at Barry to see if he was surviving this assault on his manhood. We had lived with the pink bathroom for two years.

We moved on to the playroom. "I think it would be better if we could get rid of all the toys somehow. Is that a problem?" she asked.

"It's a playroom," I said. "You would expect toys in a playroom, wouldn't you?"

"We can disguise the fact that you consider it a playroom and make it more generic," she said. "If the chalkboard stays, we'll just wipe it clean."

"No!" I said more vehemently than I meant to. "That message stays." I looked at the remnant of my son's last lemonade stand and his sweet message: "Christian's Deluxe Lemonade. $1, Free If You're Broke."

"All right," she said in a tone one would use to pacify someone who is holding hostages. "That can stay."

We went room by room until this energized realtor had swept her marketing eye over every square inch of our house, her helpful comments dripping like battery acid on my soul. After she left I said to Barry, "Who knew we had so little taste?"

We had wanted for some time to sell our house, but we live in an area of Nashville where there is a lot of new construction. Many families want to move into a brand new house with no remnants of a previous family or their pets. But our house was simply too big for us. It was the second home we had owned in that area. The first one we bought after my mother-in-law, Eleanor, died. William, my father-in-law, sold his home of more than forty years in Charleston, South Carolina, and we began to look together for a new home that would be for the four of us.

Barry fell in love with a house that had enough space to accommodate our office, too—and no pink bathroom! The appeal of staying in his pajamas till noon was overwhelmingly attractive to him. We made an offer and moved into what proved to be *the house from a very hot place that rhymes with bell.* The first time it really rained, water poured through the roof and flooded the kitchen, turning the hardwood floors into an ice rink. William appeared at breakfast one morning and announced that the ceiling above his bath was now *in* his bath. The first time we turned the water sprinklers on to irrigate the lawn, the jets shot right over the grass and into the house. I called the builder *again* and told him that the sprinklers were shooting eight feet into the house.

"Yep, that's too much," he said. He was the master of the understatement. Disaster followed disaster and finally, after discussions between attorneys, the person we originally bought the house from bought it back and moved in. We had to find a new home quickly.

When we had first looked at houses, Barry loved the house three doors down from Disaster Acres, but it was too expensive. Then we discovered that it was still for sale a year later, and it had significantly dropped in price (perchance because of the pink bathroom?). My main concern was the size. It was a big house. At that point, William had just died, so it was Barry, Christian, my assistant, Martie, and me in our office. Still, the house was a great price and interest rates were at an all-time low, so we bought it.

It never really felt like home to me, though. Barry loves vaulted ceilings and huge rooms. I prefer cozy rooms. The only thing that was cozy was the powder room in the hall, so it became my private retreat. The master bedroom was downstairs and all the rest of the bedrooms were upstairs, which made Christian nervous.

"If I need you in the night, you'll never hear me! What if a mountain lion breaks in and attacks me? I'll be on my own!" he said with customary dramatic flair.

"We don't have mountain lions in Nashville," I reasoned.

"What if one is on vacation?" he offered.

"Usually those on vacation are not aggressive," I replied. I saw his point, though. We are a very close family (our friends call us the Velcro family). So we put a makeshift bed for him in the corner of our room, which was the size of a small country and had its own zip code, until we could come up with a better plan.

## For Our Family, Less Is More

That Christmas we went to stay with my mom in Scotland. She lives in a charming stone cottage on the street where she was born. I watched the impact of her warm and inviting environment on our little unit, and it was clear to me that we would do better in a smaller house. (You know, one where you don't have to leave a trail of bread crumbs to find your way back to the kitchen.)

Barry and I talked and decided to sell. We chose a local husband-and-wife realtor team with a wonderful reputation and began the process. They offered to send another realtor over who had an eye for how to dress a home to make it sell. She was actually very sweet and helpful.

"You don't have to do any of the things I suggest. I just want to help you sell your house. You can even keep the pink bathroom!" she said with a wink.

Weeks turned into months with no offer. As our 2003 season kicked in, I was happy to let it rest for a while—we were so busy. Thanksgiving came and went, and as Christmas approached we took the house off the market until the holidays were over. We had decided to stay home that year, since we had spent the previous Christmas with Mom. I was very excited about the thought of picking out a tree, but Barry said that he and Christian would go and get it—it would be a guy thing. He said they would haul it home like two wilderness men.

I said, "Well, fie, fie then. I will just sit here on my fainting couch till y'all get back."

Lily Tomlin once said, "I've always wanted to be somebody, but I see now I should have been more specific."

The same sentiment applies when one asks one's husband to get a nice big tree. Barry and Christian spent hours examining every tree that was for sale east of the Mississippi. They assured me that they had found the perfect one, but my two wilderness men had decided to have it delivered that evening. I should have seen that as a clue as to what we were about to receive, but I didn't.

I was running Christian's bath when he came in and announced, "It's here, Mom! Our perfect tree is here. You'll love it!"

What can I say? Several things were immediately clear.

1. Either the tree could live there, or we could. There was not room for both. It was more than fourteen feet tall.

2.   A large, rabid bear could be hiding in the tree, and we wouldn't notice unless he started singing.

3.   Next year I get the tree.

I took photos of the tree and posted them on our Web site so that our family and friends could see for themselves. It was a beast. It was the tree that ate Tennessee! Barry said, "It looks a bit bigger here than it did in the lot." For four days we just circled it and stared.

Finally we moved in and attacked. It looked lovely—big, but lovely. I could not believe how much water it needed to survive. Every day I had to crawl underneath the branches and fill up the water dish. I just knew that any day I would emerge with a squirrel on my head. I mentioned that to Christian so he insisted on being there for the daily ritual; he didn't want to miss the sight of his mom with a creature in her highlights! Every night when we turned the lights on, power dipped in the whole of Tennessee.

Christmas passed; the tree died and left a thick blanket of needles on the hardwood floors. Then New Year was behind us, and we put the For Sale sign up once more. I gave the realtors a few blackout dates, such as the day of Janice's party, but basically we were open for business. I prayed that it would sell in January or February before we got busy, but there were no offers. We dropped the price. We even painted the pink bathroom green, but nothing happened.

Our conferences started in full swing. Our national conference came and went, and by then we were traveling every weekend. Barry and I prayed that if God wanted it to sell, He would bring the right buyer at the right time. I decided to forget about the house and continued working on my manuscript.

I was making good progress and learning a lot as I was writing. Janice and Brandon's e-mails kept me accountable to the harsh reality of life and yet deeply aware of the presence of God in the midst of joy and sorrow. Then we flew to San Jose for a sticker-filled day and a computerless night. My computer bag felt very light on that return flight.

"What are you going to do now, Mom?" Christian asked.

"I'll start at the beginning again," I said. "Do you think I could just leave one hundred pages blank and tell people it's for quiet personal reflection?"

"No, but you could tell them it was for coloring," he suggested.

## THE GOOD NEWS AND THE BAD NEWS

I woke up on that following Monday morning ready to dig into my book when our realtor called.

"I have good news and bad news," he said.

"Just give me the good news, and I'll get Barry for the bad," I said.

"Well they kind of go hand in hand," he replied.

"Okay—shoot!" I said as I sat down.

"We have an offer on your home."

"That's great," I said. "What's the bad?"

"You have to be out by the twenty-seventh."

"The twenty-seventh of what?" I asked.

"Of May," he whispered.

"What year?" I pressed.

"Seventeen days from now."

After two rounds of "Abide with Me," I told Barry. He seemed undeterred by the thought.

"We can do this!" he said, looking strangely like a used car salesman.

"Where will we go?" I asked.

"We'll move into an apartment for a few months until we decide what to do," he said.

"We have two conferences during the next seventeen days," I reminded him, but he was already online, researching apartments. For the next few days I did nothing on my book. I just went through our *stuff*.

Since we wanted to downsize, this seemed an ideal opportunity for a giant cleanout. Christian's school was hosting a garage sale to fund a summer mission trip, so I began taking carloads of stuff to the collecting area. After the ninth trip, one of the men responsible for arranging the donated items informed me that we as a family did not have to single-handedly fund the entire mission! He had no idea what a gift from God the timing of this sale was for our family.

I also gave furniture to friends, toys and clothes to friends with children younger than Christian, suits and shoes to girlfriends, and two desks to our church. What a huge relief. I packed and cleaned and packed and cleaned. Barry rented two apartments; a one bedroom for the office, and a two bedroom for us. The only hitch was that Martie's apartment would be ready when we moved out, but ours would not be ready until the following week. We had to find a place for four days that would accommodate our family and Belle, our bichon frise puppy.

Kathy Troccoli was kind enough to invite us to stay with her, but as I thought back on the lovely evening we had enjoyed just a few months before, celebrating her new, freshly decorated home, I couldn't imagine the Walsh troop descending upon it. We are higher maintenance than we look. We found a hotel that would take us for two of the nights, but it was booked for the first two nights because President Bush was visiting Nashville.

Then Christian came up with an idea. "Let's sleep on the floor in Miss Martie's office. It'll be like we're camping! How cool will that be?"

So that's what we did. A campout! We got out our sleeping bags, some pillows, and a lava lamp that Christian won at Chuck E. Cheese's pizza place and set up camp in the closet! Just as we were getting ready to settle in that first night, I saw that Barry was removing something from underneath the sleeping bag.

"What's that?" I asked.

"Oh, nothing," Barry replied, not wanting to alarm our son.

Christian moved in for a better look. "It's a spider, Dad," he said calmly.

I screamed and made Christian jump so that he banged his knee on the closet door. As he lay on the sleeping bag nursing this new bruise I looked at Barry, who was still standing there quietly holding the spider, and said at the top of my voice, "You so overreacted!"

Christian and his dad looked at each other and burst out laughing.

I think I even heard a little chuckle coming from the arachnid in his hand. An hour later, after we had examined every inch of the bedding, we decided it was safe to turn in.

I kept thinking of Luci Swindoll's lifelong attitude that we should treat every turn in the road as an adventure. As I lay on the floor with Barry and Christian fast asleep beside me and Belle lying across my head like earmuffs, I kept muttering over and over, "This is an adventure. This is an adventure!"

We all actually slept well on the floor for the two nights, and then we moved into the Loews Vanderbilt Hotel under the welcoming banner of their We Love Pets program. When we checked into our room, we found a little mat and a bag of treats for Belle. I had not reckoned, however, with the challenge of taking Belle to do her business while staying in a hotel. I am used to her looking at me and standing by the back door at home. Those days, she looked at me and stood at the door of our room several floors up. That first morning we hurried to the elevator with me whispering in her ear, "Not yet, not yet!"

I stood outside at five o'clock in my pajamas, trying to keep her on the four square feet of grass that the hotel provided for doggy business. The hotel is right on one of the busiest roads in Nashville. I know we must have looked like quite a sideshow.

## CUBICLE, SWEET CUBICLE

Two days later, the moving truck arrived at our new apartment to unload our stuff. I hadn't seen it yet, as I'd been busy packing the day Barry went to check it out. I wanted to get Christian out of the way of the movers, so in the morning before we got the keys, I took him over to play with his friend, Jack. By the time I got back, the movers were in full swing. I climbed up the three flights of stairs and popped my head inside.

All I could see was a tidal wave of boxes piled on top of each other. I thought, *Boy, this is a lot smaller than I thought. I'm sure it will look bigger when the boxes are out.* We worked like maniacs all day because we were leaving the next morning for our conference in Des Moines, Iowa. We piled empty box upon box just outside the front door, knowing that we had to get them to the trash compactor before the morning—there is a fine of fifty dollars for every piece of trash left in the corridor overnight.

By midnight we were almost done. That's when the storm blew in. Thunder shook our newly hung pictures, and lightning showed us how much space we didn't have, even with the boxes gone. The rain battered down as poor Barry dragged our boxes away. At one o'clock in the morning we sat down opposite each other in our living room, knees touching across the small space, and said, "Cozy, isn't it?"

I discovered that I could plug the vacuum cleaner into one outlet and clean the whole apartment. That's small! The next morning we left for Des Moines. It was a wonderful conference. When we returned, I prepared myself for an all out write-a-thon. I decided just to take the dog out for a walk first. As I lay on the ground after falling off the sidewalk, Belle lying beside me in confused solidarity, I thought, *Perhaps I should be a comedienne instead.*

## Separate Incidents with a Strong Connection

So now I sit in my local coffee shop with my surgical boot on and think back over the events that have taken place over the last few weeks: grand larceny in San Jose, Janice's e-mail, Brandon's car crash, and our family's uprooting. These events, as I have said, seemed unconnected, but I couldn't escape the conviction that they were deeply linked. The loss of my computer and our move are really only inconveniences, whereas the roads that Janice and Brandon travel have had devastating consequences for them, their families, and their finances.

My point in linking them is simply this: this is life. Life is full of minor inconveniences and the occasional disaster; where is our faith in the midst of it all?

I don't know where you find yourself as you read this book. You may be in a time where life seems to be smooth sailing. You may be facing the kind of circumstances that seem huge until you compare them to the events occurring in someone else's life—then you realize that you have little to complain about. You may be in the worst days of your life right now, crying out, "Where are You, God?"

Wherever you are, my prayer for us as we travel through these pages together is that God, by His Holy Spirit, will give us a fresh understanding of faith—of what it is and what it is not. My prayer is that He will strengthen each one of us to love and serve Him better in the days ahead. As we begin to look at faith together, I am reminded of Psalm 27. This psalm has been a rock to my soul through many difficult days.

> The LORD is my light and my salvation;
> Whom shall I fear?
> The LORD is the strength of my life;
> Of whom shall I be afraid?
> When the wicked came against me
> To eat up my flesh,
> My enemies and foes,
> They stumbled and fell.
> Though an army may encamp against me,
> My heart shall not fear;
> Though war may rise against me,
> In this I will be confident.
> One thing I have desired of the LORD,
> That will I seek:
> That I may dwell in the house of the LORD
> All the days of my life,
> To behold the beauty of the LORD,
> And to inquire in His temple.
> For in the time of trouble
> He shall hide me in His pavilion;
> In the secret place of His tabernacle
> He shall hide me;
> He shall set me high upon a rock. (vv. 1–5 NKJV)

# CHAPTER 4

# MUSTARD-SEED FAITH

## *When We Fix Our Eyes on Jesus*

∽

*Give me the faith which can remove*
*And sink the mountain to a plain;*
*Give me the childlike praying love,*
*Which longs to build Thy house again;*
*Thy love, let it my heart overpower,*
*And all my simple soul devour.*
　　　　　　　—Charles Wesley

*And when they had come to the multitude, a man came to Him, kneeling down to Him and saying, "Lord, have mercy on my son, for he is an epileptic and suffers severely; for he often falls into the fire and often into the water. So I brought him to Your disciples, but they could not cure him."*

*Then Jesus answered and said, "O faithless and perverse generation, how long shall I be with you? How long shall I bear with you? Bring him here to Me." And Jesus rebuked the demon, and it came out of him; and the child was cured from that very hour.*

*Then the disciples came to Jesus privately and said, "Why could we not cast it out"?*

*So Jesus said to them, "Because of your unbelief; for assuredly, I say to you, if you have faith as a mustard seed, you will say to this mountain, 'Move from here to there,' and it will move; and nothing will be impossible for you."*
　　　　　　　—Matthew 17:14–20 NKJV

*M*ost of my time is taken up with Women of Faith. We are on the road about thirty weekends each year, so I don't have many opportunities to take part in local church events. Once, though, a certain woman was determined to change that. She was so persistent in calling Barry year after year that in 2002 he finally said, "I think we should accept the invitation to her church conference in Pittsboro, North Carolina. I don't think this woman will quit!"

After being with WOF for six years, this was a very different experience for me. I took my place on the platform and opened with prayer. As I looked down at the program lying on the podium, I discovered that I was the worship team, then the speaker; then the soloist and the speaker again. I was the one who announced lunch and told them when lunch was over. Then once more I led worship, spoke, sang a solo, spoke again, and closed in prayer. I was very relieved to discover that I didn't have to put the chairs away! I am used to being part of a team of five speakers, a dramatist, a worship team, soloists, and an emcee. In Pittsboro I was all of the above. It was quite an adventure.

Actually we had a great time, and Barry and I felt a strong connection to those women and promised to come back the following year. In March of 2003, we returned. That first year we stayed in a small bed-and-breakfast establishment, but in 2003, Sharon, our hostess, booked Barry, Christian, Martie, and me into a beautiful hotel that was a renovated farmhouse way out in the countryside. Christian was fascinated by the breed of Scottish cows they still have on the property, the Belted Galloway. They are large black cows with a wide white stripe across their backs. He said that they looked like Oreos with legs!

Christian and Martie, who had come along to take care of Christian until we found a new nanny, decided to spend the day at the farm while we were at the church. They embarked on a scavenger hunt, gathering rocks and stones to add to his collection. When we returned that night, I discovered that they had gathered enough to build a small house!

The conference ran all day Saturday. This time the church provided a worship team and soloists, and I spoke for four sessions. I'm used to having thirty-five minutes to speak, so four hours was a little intimidating and quite a luxury. It was very moving to see what God accomplished in our lives through that day. I talked about the heartache that we attempt to hide from God and from one another and shared my own struggle with clinical depression.

At lunchtime a few volunteers handed out cards and pencils, and I asked the women to write out whatever they felt shamed by or could not break free from. At the end of the day I invited anyone who wanted to give those wounds to Jesus Christ to come and leave her card on the altar. One by one, the women streamed to the front. Some stayed for a while, weeping at the foot of the cross, while others left the cards with great joy. It was a sweet and memorable day full of fresh faith and new hope. I had no idea that my son was having a very different experience in a field just a few miles away!

That night Barry, Christian, Martie, and I had dinner at the inn's gourmet restaurant. The menu was exquisite, but I wasn't sure what to order for Christian. The food was very rich and exotic, and many of the listed meats came from animals he thought of as pets. Before the waiter took our orders, he brought tiny cups of a clear broth and some bread. By the time the waiter returned, Christian had decided that it was the only thing edible on the whole menu, so he held up his empty cup and said, "I would like six more of these, please." He obviously needed the sustenance to deliver his next weighty proclamation.

As he was downing his fifth cup of broth, he said, "Mom, did you know that there are bits in the Bible that don't work?"

"No, I didn't," I replied, wondering what was coming. "Which 'bits' are you thinking of?"

"Have you ever read that if you have faith the size of a mustard seed, you could move a mountain?" he asked.

"Yes, I know that passage."

"Well, it doesn't work," he said very seriously. "I tried."

I looked at Martie, hoping she could fill in the blanks. "He tried to move the hills this afternoon," she explained. "We read that passage in his kids' Bible this morning, and he thought that he'd start with the hills in Pittsboro."

"I wanted to move them behind the cows, Mom," he said. "I thought they would look better behind the cows. I told them and told them, but nothing moved! Actually that's not quite true. One of the cows moved, but no hills. I tried all afternoon. It was a disaster!"

We all laughed, but I empathized with Christian. I want my Christian life to be like that too. I want to understand everything. I want to know exactly what God means in every Bible passage, and I want to know that if I will do A, then God will do B. Jesus' words to His disciples are very compelling: "If you have faith as a mustard seed, you will say to this mountain, 'Move from here to there,' and it will move; and nothing will be impossible for you" (Matt. 17:20 NKJV).

That seems pretty straightforward and doable, don't you think? After all, mustard seeds are very small. I had one as a child. It was in a little glass ball that I wore on a chain around my neck. It was a tiny, unimpressive looking offering; it wasn't even a pretty seed or a perfect shape. But I remember as a little girl doing exactly what Christian did and trying to slide the Carrick Hills into the sea. Fortunately for those who love the geography of the west coast of Scotland, my faith did not prevail.

## The Least Likely to Succeed

After my conversation with Christian, I began to look at this passage in Matthew again. I wanted to help him with his dilemma, and I wanted to glean further understanding for myself.

The word used for "mustard seed" in the New Testament is the Egyptian word *sinapi*. It refers to a plant that begins as a very tiny seed, but if planted in good, fertile soil, it grows to ten or twelve feet. In Matthew 13 Jesus said that the mustard seed, although it is the least of all seeds, grows above all other herbs and offers shelter for the birds of the air. That's quite a bit of progress from such small beginnings.

The image is of something that begins as *least likely to succeed* and yet, if placed in the right environment, it will outgrow all the more impressive seeds around it. That doesn't immediately offer me or my son great comfort. Does that mean that I don't have faith as big as the smallest seed of all? If I had this tiny amount of faith, I would be able to tell the mountains to move, but so far, both my son and I are topographically inept. Jesus referred to mustard-seed faith twice in the book of Matthew, once in Mark, and twice in Luke's gospel. Each instance gives us a different picture of faith.

In Luke 17, Jesus linked faith like a mustard seed not to healing, as in Matthew 17, but to forgiveness. "If your brother sins, rebuke him, and if he repents, forgive him. If he sins against you seven times in a day, and seven times comes back to you and says, 'I repent,' forgive him."

The disciples responded by asking Jesus to give them more faith for this seemingly impossible task. Jesus responded, "If you have faith as small as a mustard seed, you can say to this mulberry tree, 'Be uprooted and planted in the sea,' and it will obey you" (Luke 17:3–4, 6).

As I read those words in the context of forgiveness, I find it easier to understand. It seems as if Jesus is saying, "Use the faith you have. Don't search for great faith, but if you love Me, use what is in you."

We know as believers that we are called to forgive. If we are called to do that, then it must be possible by the power of the Holy Spirit. Healing is a tough issue to wrestle with. I believe with all my heart that Christ still heals His people, but I have been part of many prayer meetings where, no matter how fervently we prayed or trusted God, He has not healed as we asked. When I am asked to pray for healing for someone, I always welcome that privilege, but I leave the results to God.

At a conference in 2004, Barry brought a woman to the front of the line at my book table and asked me to listen to her story. She told me that several years ago, when I was cohost of *The 700 Club*, I had prayed in faith one morning for someone in our viewing audience God had shown me. This person was incapacitated as a singer because of nodes on her vocal cords. She told me that as I prayed, God healed her completely. I am very humbled by stories like this and convinced that God uses the tiniest fragment of faith to do His great work. This story makes me thankful to God, but I have to tell you that I have prayed for many more people who have not been healed. God holds the keys to these mysteries.

If healing is a divisive issue denominationally, forgiveness is clear to every follower of Christ. Those of us who have been forgiven of our sins must forgive others. So rather than being preoccupied with the spectacular, i.e., moving a mountain, the call is to use the faith that is in us as believers and live as believers and followers of Christ should live.

## MUSTARD SEEDS AND THE KINGDOM OF GOD

In Matthew 13 and Mark 4, Jesus used the mustard seed to describe the kingdom of God.

> He told them another parable: "The kingdom of heaven is like a mustard seed, which a man took and planted in his field. Though it is the smallest of all your seeds, yet when it grows, it is the largest of garden plants and becomes a tree, so that the birds of the air come and perch in its branches." (Matt.13:31–32)

> Again he said, "What shall we say the kingdom of God is like, or what parable shall we use to describe it? It is like a mustard seed, which is the smallest seed you plant in the ground." (Mark 4:30–31)

It seems as if Jesus was telling His disciples that although His ministry appeared to be starting small, it would become a place of refuge for all who sought shelter. Many looked at Christ's humility and underestimated His strength. Even those closest to Him wanted a greater show of power.

In Luke 13 Jesus healed a woman who had been crippled for eighteen years. The Pharisees were furious that He performed this miracle on the Sabbath. They said there were six days to be healed, but they should not look for healing on that one holy day. Jesus criticized their hypocrisy, telling them that if they had a valuable possession, such as a donkey that fell into a well on the Sabbath, they would pull it free. So why withhold the goodness of God from this broken woman for one more day?

When you look at all the references to mustard-seed faith together, the picture becomes a little clearer. The kingdom, the work of God in our hearts, begins as a small seed, but as it is placed in good soil—the Word of God, prayer, fellowship—it grows and offers shelter to others.

I have been a follower of Christ since I was eleven years old. I have never consciously rebelled against God or been out of fellowship with Him, but I am overwhelmed by my lack of the kind of faith that could move mountains or perform great miracles pointing to our Father. Perhaps the mountains Christ referred to are not quite as I have imagined.

## A Different Kind of Mountain

One of the next things I noted, after looking at the image of the mustard seed, was that the object Jesus suggested our faith could move in Matthew 17 was a mountain, not a tree or an ocean. If you study the references to mountains in the Old Testament, they are often linked with the promise that God will clear a path for us, He will help us overcome great hardship, and He will make our way straight.

In the book of Isaiah, we read of the role of John the Baptist and the coming Messiah:

"A voice of one calling: 'In the desert prepare the way for the LORD; make straight in the wilderness a highway for our God. Every valley shall be raised up, every mountain and hill made low; the rough ground shall become level, the rugged places a plain'" (Isa. 40:3–4).

Again in 49:11: "I will turn all my mountains into roads, and my highways will be raised up."

In 54:10, the image reveals that even if everything around us is shaking, God's love will not be moved: "'Though the mountains be shaken and the hills be removed, yet my unfailing love for you will not be shaken nor my covenant of peace be removed,' says the LORD, who has compassion on you."

As I read and studied further, it seemed clear that Jesus used the enormity of a mountain to show how God moves on behalf of His people. I love the contrast of what we bring to the table and how God responds. We bring a fragment of faith, and God moves a mountain!

My friend Janice faces mountain after mountain, and I am sure that at times she feels as if she has no faith left. Yet she takes one more step . . . then another. I find her words to me remarkable: "One more thing gone wrong, one more prescription to take with all the other drugs. The 'other' problems combined with the cancer make this battle seem almost insurmountable. Almost."

There it is; that tiny seed wrapped up in one word: *almost*.

Perhaps as you look at your own life, you feel as if you have no faith at all, and yet here you are. You picked up a book on faith, you took a small step, perhaps out of curiosity, even cynicism, but you still took the step. I think again of Mary Graham's words that faith is not about our mustering up huge reserves of mountain-moving power but about leaning on Christ, trusting our Father, and taking one more step. We start with what we have. We bring the tiniest seed of faith that God has placed in our spirits, and God honors that faith. If we spend our time looking at the mountain, we will be overwhelmed, so we nurture the seed that God has planted in us.

I received a letter from a woman who wanted to talk to her neighbor about Jesus but felt overwhelmed at the thought of leading another to faith. I asked her, "What seems doable to you?"

"I could invite her in for coffee," she suggested.

"That's a great beginning," I said.

After that she wrote and told me that she believed she could invite her neighbor to a concert at her church. Then when the neighbor responded warmly to that, she invited her to a Sunday service. A few weeks later, the neighbor gave her life to Christ.

My point is, start where you are and leave the rest up to God. Just take the first step.

I see that kind of faith in Christian too. That kind of faith took him all the way up the wall to ring the bell at the top.

## ONE MORE STEP

About three years ago Nashville was graced with a large outlet mall, Opry Mills. We avoided it for the first few months, as the crowds were overwhelming. Then I called one of the restaurants, Rainforest Cafe, to make a reservation.

"We don't take reservations. You just have to come and get in line," the chirpy voice announced.

"How long is the wait?" I asked.

"Four to five hours," he said.

"So, basically you have to get in line when you're not hungry, knowing that you'll be starving when it's your turn?" I suggested.

He laughed and encouraged me to have an earth-friendly day!

Finally we decided to brace ourselves and explore the mall. One of the first things that Christian saw was a rock-climbing wall inside a sports store. "Can I do it, Mom? Please, please, please!"

I took in the huge wall and my little boy and heard a million and one warnings bubble to the surface.

*He'll fall!*

*He'll poke his eye out!*

*It's all fun and games until someone gets hurt!*

I looked at Barry, and he stepped into the breach. "Let's check it out," he said.

I read the sheet that parents had to sign relinquishing the store of all responsibility when Christian's rope snapped and he plummeted to the ground, poking his eye out on the way down! Barry signed, and we got in line. When it was his turn, a lanky teenager strapped him into a harness.

"Are the harnesses new?" I asked.

"It's cool, dude," he replied. "You can sit over there."

So *dude* took a seat.

Christian started to climb. At one point he stopped and looked back at us. "I'm doing it! I'm doing it!" he cried. There was such a look of pure, unadulterated joy at his achievement. As he got closer to the top, however, he faltered. He looked for Barry. "I don't think I can go any farther," he said.

"That's cool, Christian. You've done great. Do you want to come down now?" Barry asked.

"I don't really want to, but I'm afraid."

"Then just take one more step," Barry coached.

Christian took one more and stopped. Then he took another. I sat and watched as he calculated each deliberate step. Sometimes he waited for a while, but then he moved again. In just a few moments he was at the top, and he reached out and rang the bell. I don't think Olympic athletes could feel more pride as the gold medals are placed around their necks than my son felt that day: "Did you see me, Mom? Did you hear the bell? Did I look cool? Did you see when I almost plunged to the earth?"

Yes!

Yes!

Yes!

What!!!

Christian's experience that day seemed to me to be a reflection of the Christian life and the place of faith. We start well, we falter, we almost turn around—but we don't want to, for where else would we go? So we take one more step, just one more little step even though the journey is almost too much for us—*almost*.

## FAITH DEFINED?

"Now faith is the substance of things hoped for, the evidence of things not seen" (Heb. 11:1 NKJV). Throughout the whole canon of Scripture, we have the preceding fifteen words offered to us as the only definition of faith. In other passages we have pictures of those who *exhibited faith*, what it looks like to *break faith*, constant exhortations to *have faith* or *stand firm in the faith,* to *live by faith,* rebukes of those with *little faith,* those who are rewarded *because of their faith,* and those who will *turn away from their faith.* But Hebrews 11:1 is the only actual definition of what the content of faith looks like.

In his marvelous book *The Pursuit of God,* A. W. Tozer writes, "In Scripture there is practically no effort made to define faith." In referencing Hebrews 11:1 he writes, "Even there, faith is defined functionally, not philosophically: that is, it is a statement of what faith is *in operation,* not what it is *in essence.*"

When the writer to the Hebrews offered his definition, he presented it to us as a *present* reality, not a *pursued* reality. By that I mean he wrote assuming that the reader already has faith. There is great significance in that. Faith is something to be experienced and exercised, not defined, categorized, and neatly packaged. If you asked my friend Janice to define faith, I'm not sure she would be able, to her satisfaction, to put into words the very life force that is holding her up moment by moment. If you sat down with Chris and Jan Harris and asked them to write out a definition of faith as they have walked through the nightmare of their son's accident and subsequent recovery, I am sure that words on paper would never weigh the same as the spiritual treasure they carry in their hearts, having watched the work of God in Brandon's life.

Tozer shares his experience of faith as "the gaze of a soul upon a saving God." I love that!

That is what I want for my son. That is what I long to pursue in my own life. That is what I see in Janice, in Jan and Chris and Brandon. That is what I pray for you. That encapsulates the truth that having faith, again, is not about you or me mustering up enough faith to shift the Swiss Alps left a bit, but, rather, facing our own mountains in life, gazing upon God, who is the only One who can save us. There is a very clear show-and-tell of what that would look like in a physical reality in the journey of the children of Israel toward the promised land. They had rebelled against God time and time again, but His faithfulness to them was endless.

## SIGN OF THE SNAKE

Numbers is the fourth book Moses wrote. It chronicles the events right before God's people took possession of the promised land. It's not a book people often choose for personal Bible study, as the long lists of names and numbers can be more intimidating than inspiring. To Moses and his people, though, they were a testimony of the faithfulness of God through trying and devastating times.

The book is roughly divided into two sections, and each one begins with a census. The first took place in Sinai during the second year that the children of Israel spent in the wilderness. Every man more than twenty years of age was counted. This first generation of God's people should have entered and enjoyed the promised land, but due to their rebellion and disbelief, God found them faithless. He allowed them to live out their lives in the desert but never to cross into the land that their children would possess. They were able only to see their children grow up and to embrace their grandchildren, only to touch the faces of those who would inherit the promise of God in their places.

The second section in Numbers took place almost forty years later. It is a list of those who were then ready to march into all that God had promised them. When Moses, and Eleazar the priest (Aaron's son and the nephew of Moses), counted all the men more than twenty years old, every one of the men on the first census had died save two, Caleb and Joshua. From chapter 26 to the end, we read of the preparations the people made to begin the march.

The passage I want us to look at gives us a picture of faith as *gazing at God*. It took place with the first group of people in the desert, those who left Egypt and crossed the Red Sea but never made it all the way home. The story appears in chapter 21.

> They traveled from Mount Hor along the route to the Red Sea, to go around Edom. But the people grew impatient on the way; they spoke against God and against Moses, and said, "Why have you brought us up out of Egypt to die in the desert? There

is no bread! There is no water! And we detest this miserable food!"

Then the Lord sent venomous snakes among them; they bit the people and many Israelites died. The people came to Moses and said, "We sinned when we spoke against the Lord and against you. Pray that the Lord will take the snakes away from us." So Moses prayed for the people.

The Lord said to Moses, "Make a snake and put it up on a pole; anyone who is bitten can look at it and live." So Moses made a bronze snake and put it up on a pole. Then when anyone was bitten by a snake and looked at the bronze snake, he lived. (vv. 4–9)

I often find the violence and judgment in the Old Testament hard to understand. We live under the banner of the grace of God and the new covenant. But even in God's harshest judgments, we can see His mercy again and again.

## FOREVER FAITHFUL

His patience with the Israelites was remarkable. Remember what He had brought them from: they had lived through the plagues that fell upon Pharaoh and the Egyptians. They had been spared on that night when the angel of death passed over the blood-soaked door-posts of the Israelites but took the life of every firstborn son of the Egyptians. They had seen the Red Sea part to make a path for them—a path that closed behind them, taking the lives of those who hounded them. They had seen Moses, his face shining with a brilliance no man or woman had witnessed before, because he had seen the glory of God when he received the Ten Commandments for the second time. They ate fresh food that was dropped from heaven every day. They followed a pillar of cloud as they traveled during the day and were led by fire at night.

As a woman I find it very moving to discover the faithfulness of

God to the women of that time and culture. You will see, if you read the passages that detail the taking of the census, each time only the men are counted. What about the women? What about those whose fathers had died and they were unmarried? Who would take care of them when the land was divided up?

Five sisters were in that situation (Num. 27). They approached Moses and asked that they be allowed to take inheritance of the portion of land that would have been their father's. This was unheard of— women were not allowed by law to be landowners. Moses took the matter to God. I love the pattern beginning to be apparent: when a question arose on a new issue, the response was to go to God for an answer. God told Moses that the women had presented a just cause and would indeed inherit their father's portion of the land. That might not seem like a significant event in our culture, but it was a breakthrough in their times, and another picture of God's faithfulness.

God's people had seen miracle after miracle and still openly rebelled: "Why have you brought us up out of Egypt to die in the desert? There is no bread! There is no water! And we detest this miserable food!" I often remember this passage when I am tempted to think that if I saw a tangible, physical miracle, I would have greater faith. Miracles don't seem to have the effect of increasing faith; faith seems to be the gift we receive by gazing at the face of God. Scripture is full of examples of those who witnessed incredible miracles, but their hearts were not changed.

The children of Israel watched as God caused the Red Sea to divide before their eyes, but it didn't change them.

Judas watched as Christ fed the masses with a boy's lunch, and it didn't change him.

The disciples saw Jesus call Lazarus back from death to life, but they still didn't understand that Christ ruled over death. They fled in despair when Christ was arrested.

Think of times in your own life when God has answered a specific prayer or intervened in a miraculous way. Did that change you, or did it draw you closer to God?

## FAITH CALLS US TO LOOK UP

You might be wondering how this passage relates to us today. To answer that, let's go to John's gospel. In chapter 3 we have the story of Jesus' encounter with Nicodemus. Nicodemus was a prominent Pharisee, a respected member of the ruling council. He came at night to ask Jesus a question. It is obvious from his opening salutation that he held Christ in high regard:

"Rabbi, we know you are a teacher who has come from God. For no one could perform the miraculous signs you are doing if God were not with him" (v. 2).

Jesus' reply cut right through Nicodemus's preamble to the heart of the matter: "I tell you the truth, no one can see the kingdom of God unless he is born again" (v. 3). The metaphor confused Nicodemus, so he asked how such a thing was possible. Jesus turned the question back to him and asked how it was possible to be such a highly regarded teacher and yet have so little understanding. Then He took Nicodemus right to the passage in Numbers: "Just as Moses lifted up the snake in the desert, so the Son of Man must be lifted up, that everyone who believes in him may have eternal life" (v. 14–15).

Only those who looked up at the bronze snake in Moses' hand were spared. The others died. Faith here is a call to look up, to gaze at our Savior. Faith is a passionate gaze at the only One who can save us. Think of the many times in Scripture that picture is used.

Lift up your heads, O you gates;
    be lifted up, you ancient doors,
      that the King of glory may come in. (Ps. 24:7)

I lift up my eyes to the hills—
    where does my help come from? (Ps. 121:1)

When these things begin to take place, stand up and lift up your heads, because your redemption is drawing near. (Luke 21:28)

Perhaps the greatest call to gaze on our Lord appears right after the great faith chapter of Hebrews 11:

> Therefore, since we are surrounded by such a great cloud of witnesses, let us throw off everything that hinders and the sin that so easily entangles, and let us run with perseverance the race marked out for us. *Let us fix our eyes on Jesus,* the author and perfecter of our faith, who for the joy set before him endured the cross, scorning its shame, and sat down at the right hand of the throne of God. (Heb. 12:1–2, emphasis added)

As I think of my son standing in a field in North Carolina trying to rearrange the scenery, I am gifted with a clear picture of why we often think as believers that we don't have enough faith. We tend to think;

If we prayed harder . . .

If we prayed in a more compelling tone . . .

If under our breaths we are whispering, "I think I can, I think I can, I think I can . . ." then we would show enough faith to receive answers to our prayers.

Faith is not wishful thinking or theatrics. Faith is born in us as we fix our eyes on Jesus and as we recognize the fingerprints of God the Father all over our lives.

If you are like me, you have been familiar with the phrase "Fix your eyes on Jesus" for some time, but you may wonder what it means, what it looks like. When I was a teenager I was stumped by Christ's command to pick up my cross every day and follow Him. I had no idea how to do that. Did it mean that I should carve up the breakfast table and drag it around the neighborhood? As I studied and prayed, I became convinced that it means that every time my will crossed God's will, I dragged my will back in line with His. It means doing the things that I know are good and true, whether I feel like it or not. It means setting my face and heart toward heaven just as Jesus did. But what about "Fix your eyes on Jesus"?

I believe that it means that we study how Jesus lived, how He loved, and follow His example. When we find ourselves in a difficult place, we do what He did: we turn to our Father.

Christian may never be able to master mountain moving, but it's my prayer that as he grows he will exercise the tiny mustard seed of faith planted in the hearts of those who love God. Then he will see God move mountains on his behalf and take him over them when they remain in place. That faith grows as we watch how God works.

Let's look at His ways.

# CHAPTER 5

# GOD'S TRACK RECORD

## *When We Recognize the Hand of God on Our Lives*

∽

*How firm a foundation, ye saints of the Lord,*
*Is laid for your faith in His excellent Word!*
*What more can He say than to you He hath said,*
*To you, who for refuge to Jesus have fled?*

*The soul that on Jesus hath leaned for repose,*
*I will not, I will not desert to his foes;*
*That soul, though all hell should endeavor to shake,*
*I'll never, no never, no never forsake!*
> —Text attributed variously to John Keene,
> Kirkham, and John Keith

*God has said,*
    *"Never will I leave you;*
    *never will I forsake you."*
*So we say with confidence,*
    *"The Lord is my helper; I will not be afraid.*
    *What can man do to me?"*
> —Hebrews 13:5–6

I put the finishing touches on the previous chapter, *saved it to a CD*, got up, stretched, and decided to take Belle for a walk (*in hoes!*). Belle has the gift of sniffing. Her whole life consists of sleeping, eating, eliminating, chewing things, and sniffing, but it seems to me she savors sniffing above all else.

Several dogs live in the apartment complex. There is another bichon, a weiner dog, two Mattipoos or Pooimalts (I can never remember how to address that combination of breeds), and the dog that Christian and I have named "Attila the Hound." Attila is a German shepherd, a breed that I like a lot, but this one has anger issues. This dog's owner is barely able to hold onto its leash. Attila drags her around, looking for new people to scare. Attila barks and growls and rears up on its back legs as if to pounce and devour at any moment. Belle is neither impressed nor intimidated. She barks back, but in a different key—a friendly key. She wags her tail and moves toward the big beast as the owner drags it away. My personal conviction is that if the owner ever let Attila go, the bark would dissipate into a whimper, but I will let that remain a theory.

I talk to Belle when we are on our walks. We discuss the weather, the scenery, and what a great dog she is. I often run my new ideas for the next chapter by her. "Did you know that God has an amazing track record with those who love Him, Belle?" I asked.

She wagged her tail in assent.

"Even with those who don't know Him, He is remarkable, merciful, and faithful."

She offered one further wag and continued sniffing the grass. We headed back and climbed the three flights of stairs to our apartment. I made a fresh pot of coffee, and as it was brewing I flicked on the television to catch the lunchtime news. Instead I was greeted by a television preacher. I was horrified by what I heard.

## LOSING A MIRACLE

This person was speaking about the faithfulness of God. She said that it is up to us as believers to muster up enough faith for a miracle, and then to keep the level of faith high enough to maintain it, or it would be taken away. I almost choked. What made it worse was that she was using Scripture to support her position.

I thought of the verse warning us, "Be self-controlled and alert. Your enemy the devil prowls around like a roaring lion looking for someone to devour. Resist him, standing firm in the faith, because you know that your brothers throughout the world are undergoing the same kind of sufferings" (1 Pet. 5:8–9).

This preacher told her audience that Satan wants to snatch our faith, our healing, away, and it was up to us to make sure that didn't happen. As the cameras panned across the faces of men and women taking notes, they nodded in assent. My heart sank with her final words before I switched it off: In essence she said, "If you've lost your healing, it's your fault!"

Do you believe that?

Do you live in fear of Satan's snatching away your faith?

If life is not working for you and those you love at the moment, do you think that it is your fault?

I don't believe that!

What I want us to do in this chapter is take a look at God's track record with one man, both when he displayed a lot of faith and when he did not. I believe that our picture of ourselves is too big, and our picture of God is too small. God is not a cruel father who takes delight in taunting His children and punishing them if their faith report card has a few low grades. Let me show you what I base that conviction on from God's Word. Let's begin by taking a look at the life of Abraham. His story is a treasure chest full of spiritual gifts for us.

## THE FATHER OF FAITH

I don't know how familiar you are with his story. Most of us raised in church know the basics. God called Abraham to leave his homeland and go to a place God would show him. He had a son, Isaac, when he was very old, and God told Abraham to offer Isaac as a sacrifice. Abraham was willing, and God spared his son. Abraham became known as the great father of the faith, but there is much more to his story. If we will take a close look at the good *and* bad choices, the moments of faith *and* of doubt or disobedience, I believe we will find many lessons for our lives today.

Abraham did not begin his journey as a follower of God. We read in Joshua 24:2, "Joshua said to all the people, 'This is what the LORD, the God of Israel, says: "Long ago your forefathers, including Terah the father of Abraham and Nahor, lived beyond the River and worshiped other gods."'" This is the first time in Scripture that we are made aware of people worshiping false gods.

At the point when we first meet him in Genesis, his name is Abram, *Avram* in Hebrew, which means "exalted father." God later changed his name to Abraham, *Avraham*, which means "father of a multitude." We don't know much about Abraham's conversion experience, just that it occurred sometime after God told him to leave his home and his relatives to go to a place God would show him. That's quite a command! *Leave everything you have, and everything you know, and follow Me.* The command, however, came with an incredible promise: "I will make you into a great nation and I will bless you; I will make your name great, and you will be a blessing. I will bless those who bless you, and whoever curses you I will curse; and all peoples on earth will be blessed through you" (Gen. 12:2–3).

Abraham went from an empty, one-sided relationship with gods who could not talk to an encounter with Jehovah, the living God, who promised him blessing, greatness, and protection.

What a promise! All that his father, Terah, passed on to him was empty, dead worship, but everything was about to change. At that point Abraham was seventy-five years old. I love the fact that the Genesis account shows the development of Abraham's faith. He started with conditional faith that grew and grew, he fell back again and again, and then he developed mature, rock-solid faith.

## FLAWED FAITH

Some commentators view Abraham's first act of responding to God's command as flawed, stating that he had been told not to take any of his father's family when he left his homeland, but he took his nephew, Lot, who had been with him from birth. Other writers believe that his obedience was complete since Lot had been part of his family from boyhood. If you take the first position, Abraham obeyed most of the command and ignored just one little detail; that is a very human flaw. Ever been there?

When Christian was five years old, we had an unusual amount of snowfall in Nashville. Barry went to the hardware store and bought two sleds, a bright orange one and a shiny blue one shaped like a saucer. We all wrapped up well and headed outside.

"I want to slide down that side of the hill, Dad," Christian said.

"No, that side is too high. But we can sled down here and here," Barry said, showing him places with a gentler incline.

We had so much fun. All the neighborhood children were out in force, and moms and dads were there to help pull sleds back up the hill, take photos, and thaw out frozen bodies with steaming hot chocolate.

"That boy did the big side of the hill," Christian said indignantly.

"That boy is ten years old," Barry said.

"I'm not having any fun!" Christian pouted.

"Well, that is your choice, young man," I said. "I'm having a lot of fun."

We pulled our sleds up to the top one more time. I took my eyes off Christian for one second, and when I looked back he was halfway down the steep side of the hill. I yelled for Barry to run around to the bottom and help him while I took off after him on my sled. I watched as my son careened to the bottom and kept going until he hit a tree and fell off, unharmed, into the snow. I caught up with him just as his dad was picking him up. Christian stood up, wiped the snow off his face, and kicked the tree!

Human beings always want to do the one thing they are told not to do. Perhaps it was that allure that pulled Adam and Eve toward the tree of the knowledge of good and evil. I have discovered in my life that God gave His laws and guidance because He loves us, not because He wants to spoil our fun.

But God is patient and faithful even when our obedience is limited.

## DECEIT IN EGYPT

So Abraham, Lot, and Abraham's wife, Sarah, packed up their belongings and their livestock and left Ur of the Chaldeans. They arrived in Canaan and pitched their tents. God spoke to Abraham again and told him that the very land he stood on, which the Canaanites currently occupied, would belong to him and to his descendants. God's promise overwhelmed Abraham, and he built an altar to the Lord.

So far, so good. Perhaps he took Lot when he should have gone alone, but things seemed to be going well.

Then a famine hit the land. Instead of asking God what to do, Abraham decided, as the head of the household, that he would take matters into his own hands and move to Egypt. I have great sympathy with this decision. Abraham was just getting to know God. He didn't know if God did food as well as land and descendants. He was responsible for his family and didn't want them to starve.

It's easy to read the Bible through critical eyes and wonder why Abraham made certain choices, but God understood and patiently worked with Abraham. What's more amazing to me is that even those of us who have the wealth of the Old and New Testaments, who live after the resurrection of Christ, who have the promised Holy Spirit to guide and lead us, still make so many bad choices or fear-filled decisions. Yet God's patience and mercy and love are available to each one of us!

So Abraham took his family out of Canaan, the place of God's promise, and they went to Egypt for food. As they were about to enter Egypt, Abraham became aware of a potential problem. He was afraid that the Egyptians might want his beautiful wife and kill him to get her. So he schemed: "Say you are my sister, so that I will be treated well for your sake and my life will be spared because of you" (Gen. 12:13).

Sarah agreed to this strange request. Just as Abraham feared, when word reached Pharaoh that a beautiful new woman was in town, he sent for her. It seemed as if Abraham's disobedience was going to destroy God's plan. Abraham and Sarah were in the wrong place with the wrong people. They were not supposed to be in Egypt. But our faithlessness never destroys God's plans.

I am often asked about the will of God. I spoke with a college student in Chicago who was consumed with fear that she had missed God's perfect will for her life because she had decided to go to a different school than the one she believed He had directed her to. "I know that God opened a door at a different school, but I wanted to be near my boyfriend. Now we're not together, and I think I've ruined my life!"

It was a joy to be able to take this young woman to so many places in God's Word where people like Abraham made wrong choices, but God's perfect will prevailed.

Still, there are consequences for our disobedience, and sometimes others must suffer them. God punished Pharaoh for Sarah's presence in his palace. When Pharaoh found out that Sarah was Abraham's wife, he was justifiably furious. "So Pharaoh summoned Abram. 'What have you done to me?' he said. 'Why didn't you tell me she was your wife? Why did you say, "She is my sister," so that I took her to be my wife? Now then, here is your wife. Take her and go!'" (Gen. 12:18–19).

(Isn't it interesting that this was the place where Abraham's descendants would live in slavery for four hundred years, until one of Pharaoh's descendants set them free and sent them out of the land?)

## CARELESS CHOICES IN CANAAN

Then Abraham, Lot, their families, staff, and livestock moved to Negev, a desert area south of Judea, and settled there. Trouble began to brew between Abraham's workers and Lot's workers. The land simply would not support that many people. (Of course, in God's plan there would have been only half as many.) So they decided the only solution was for them to part company. Abraham's next decision was another careless choice that put his future and that of his descendants in jeopardy.

He let Lot choose where he would settle. He was on the verge of giving his nephew the promised land! But Lot chose to go east to the Jordan valley, and Abraham remained in Canaan. The land that Lot chose looked spectacular, very lush and rich like Egypt, but with every step he took he was headed for disaster. Lot moved all his people, his wife, and his daughters to a place very close to the town of Sodom. It seemed as if he had made a wise choice until the king of Elam attacked Sodom and Gomorrah. In the ensuing battle, his troops captured Lot and everything he owned.

Someone got word to Abraham, and when he heard about Lot's capture he went to his nephew's aid. He took 318 men and in a surprise attack at night rescued Lot, the others held captive, and all their possessions. As Abraham was returning from this amazing victory he met two kings, the king of Sodom and Melchizedek, king of Salem.

Melchizedek was a priest of God. In Psalm 110 David referred to him: "The LORD has sworn and will not change his mind: 'You are a priest forever, in the order of Melchizedek'" (v. 4). Melchizedek was an Old Testament priest who foreshadowed the One who would come to save all God's people. He brought bread and wine to Abraham and blessed him. Abraham gave Melchizedek a tenth of everything he had brought back from battle.

In essence, Abraham received the bread and the wine and paid his tithe. I love the little pictures of the life we live today, from Omaha to Edinburgh, tucked into the pages of the Word of God.

The king of Sodom told Abraham that he could keep all the possessions he had taken in victory, including those of the king himself, but the king wanted his people back. He was offering Abraham a deal—"You take some and I'll take some." But Abraham saw the danger in accepting gifts from the king, and Abraham refused to take a thing for himself.

Do you see how faith was beginning to grow?

After Abraham's first encounter with God, he did *almost* everything

He asked but perhaps reasoned, *I'll need someone to help me reestablish in a new area, so I'll take Lot.* God let him do that, but it was a decision that made life more difficult than it needed to be. Then a wealthy king from a very pagan city offered to provide for Abraham, but he refused to accept his help, depending instead on God alone. Abraham was changing based on *who God was showing Himself to be.*

## SONLESS AND SAD

God responded to Abraham's budding faith and told him He would be his Defender and Protector. But God's goodness and the wealth of His promise, instead of being a joy and encouragement, had a negative effect on Abraham. His basic feeling was "What's the point? I have no son, so whatever You give me, my slave will inherit."

God was patient again with Abraham. He didn't rebuke him or remind him that He overlooked his last indiscretion. He spoke lovingly to him: "'A son coming from your own body will be your heir.' He took him outside and said, 'Look up at the heavens and count the stars—if indeed you can count them.' Then he said to him, 'So shall your offspring be'" (Gen. 15:4–5).

Does that sound like the heart of a God who expects us to get it all right, or He will remove His blessing and favor? God's kindness called Abraham to a new place of faith. "Abram believed the LORD, and he credited it to him as righteousness" (v. 6). The father-heart of God is so clear in His relationship with Abraham. He was patient and kind, forgiving and gentle.

Sometimes in our lives we become so discouraged that we doubt God's care. We find ourselves asking, "God, do You see me? Do You know what I long for, and does that matter to You?"

## PRAYER ON THE HILL

Barry and I went through that shortly after we were married in 1994. We were living in Laguna Beach in Southern California. Barry was working in the development department at Fuller Theological Seminary, and I was pregnant with Christian. Each day Barry's drive to and from work took three hours, courtesy of California traffic. He had tremendous respect for the seminary but didn't enjoy his work. Barry is a very creative person, and he felt stifled within the academic world. Financially, things were very tight, and with a baby on the way, that was a concern too.

Every evening after supper we climbed the hill in front of our rented house and looked out at the sunset. I knew that Barry was discouraged even though he tried to shield me from it. When we met, he had been working for a television network, a job that gave him great scope for his gifts, but he believed that God told him to leave this job. We talked about the ramifications of that as we were about to start a new life together; I, too, felt that it was the right thing to do. We thought that if he was obedient to God, then God would immediately open a new, wonderful opportunity.

That was not the case. Barry took a few temp jobs while he applied to other networks, but every door slammed in his face. Then he sat in traffic for three hours every day for a job he didn't enjoy.

"I wonder if I missed God," he said one night as we watched the evening sky.

"What do you mean?" I asked.

"I wonder if I took the wrong major in college, or if I made a mistake leaving my other job."

My heart ached for him. I could see how frustrated and miserable he was. All we could do was wait. Every evening we sat side by side on the hill, and as the sun set, our prayers rose to our Father.

We had no idea that God was about to open the door to a great adventure for our whole family through Women of Faith. Now we travel and work together. Barry is in his element working with marketing and media, the very thing that was his major in college.

Waiting is hard. We feel as if we are doing nothing, and very often we are tempted to intervene. That is what happened with Abraham and Sarah.

## TIRED OF WAITING

Abraham was about to learn a lesson that we are faced with from time to time. He was tired of waiting for God to do what He promised, so he took matters into his own hands. Ten years had passed since God's promise that Abraham would have a son—ten long years of watching his wife and her monthly disappointment. Abraham was then eighty-five years old.

Since God had not moved in the way they expected, they decided to come up with a plan of their own. It was acceptable, even expected in that time and culture that a childless couple turn to a surrogate to give them children. Sarah told Abraham to sleep with her slave girl, Hagar, who immediately became pregnant. Once more Abraham experienced the chaos that arises when we come up with our own plans apart from God's revealed will.

What *sounded* like a good plan did not *feel* like a good plan once it began to unfold. Hagar was thrilled that she was able to conceive Abraham's child so quickly and began to despise Sarah. Life became intolerable for Sarah. Not only did she have to deal with the reality that the infertility problem was obviously hers, not Abraham's, but she had to endure the disdain of her servant. It was too much for her. Sarah treated Hagar so badly that Hagar ran away.

There was discord then, too, between Sarah and Abraham as they passed blame back and forth.

> Sarai said to Abram, "You are responsible for the wrong I am suffering. I put my servant in your arms, and now that she knows she is pregnant, she despises me. May the LORD judge between you and me."
> "Your servant is in your hands," Abram said. (Gen. 16:5–6)

When chaos ensues after we abandon God's plan for our own, the natural thing to do is to blame someone else.

When I was about sixteen, my young cousins came to stay with us for two weeks. They slept in my brother's room, and Stephen moved in with my mom. Stephen told the cousins they could play with any of the toys in his bedroom except his globe, which he didn't want them to touch. One morning when my mom went in to wake them, one cousin was sitting up in bed with the globe in her hands. She looked at it, looked at my mom, and said, "This thing is in my bed again!"

It's hard to take responsibility for our own messes. As the drama unfolded between Abraham and Sarah, Hagar was facing her own battle. She was alone and pregnant and in the desert. It must have been terrifying to be so vulnerable and without help.

*What will happen to me?*

*What will happen to my child?*

*We will die out here!*

Hagar was about to experience God's faithfulness in her own life. God sent an angel to her as she sat by a stream on the road to Shur. We know from that geographical reference that Hagar was going back to Egypt. The angel asked her two questions: "Where have you come from, and where are you going?" (Gen. 16:8).

## Key Questions

Those two questions have enormous weight in our journey with God. If you find yourself feeling as if you have lost your way, these are the questions to ask:

"Lord, where have You brought me from?"

"Lord, where do You want me to go?"

Hagar told the angel that she was running away from her mistress. The angel of the Lord told her to go back to Sarah, that she would give birth to a boy, and she should call him Ishmael because God heard her crying in the desert. (The Hebrew for "Ishmael" and "has heard" are very similar.) Hagar was amazed at God's grace and favor to her. She called God *El Roi,* "the God who sees." You might feel as if God no longer sees you, but Hagar's declaration of one of the characteristics of our God is rock solid. God sees us.

God saw Hagar by the stream.

God saw Barry on the hillside.

God sees you.

Hagar returned to Sarah, and Ishmael was born. Time passed. When Abraham turned ninety-nine, God spoke to him again about His promise: "I am God Almighty; walk before me and be blameless. I will confirm my covenant between me and you and will greatly increase your numbers" (Gen. 17:1–2).

It is at this point that God changed Abram to Abraham and Sarai to Sarah. This time God was very specific! "I will bless her and will surely give you a son by her" (Gen. 17:16). In other words, "You'll be the father, and she will be the mother. Is that clear?"

Abraham just laughed. But God is faithful when we are faithless, and Abraham had quite a birthday gift as he turned one hundred years old: Sarah gave birth to Isaac.

## The Greatest Test of All

I wonder if ninety in biblical days is the forty of today. People lived such long lives then. Abraham's father, Terah, was 205 years old when he died. Just as Sarah was amazed that God would give her a son when she was sure it was too late, I, too, had a divine surprise.

Barry and I wanted to have children, and we had been trying for about a year with no results. I thought I had left it until too late. So I went to see a gynecologist. I met first with the nurse.

"How old are you?" she asked.

"Thirty-nine," I said.

"You'll be lucky," was her skeptical reply. "All your eggs are probably hard-boiled by now!"

The doctor was more optimistic, but I was discouraged. Still, I bought a couple of pregnancy test kits. I was sure we would have to try for a while.

One day as I was cleaning the bathroom I came across one of the kits and decided to take it rather than just toss it out. (I guess there was nothing worth watching on TV that morning!) I left it on the window ledge and kept cleaning.

A few hours later I saw it sitting there. Rebuking myself for this unhygienic practice, I picked it up to throw it out. Just as it fell into the trash can, I saw a little check mark. I picked it up and stared at it, then repeated the test with another kit. Again I saw that little mark. I drove to the drugstore and bought another one. Same result. I drove back again, and as I was standing in line to pay for the test, the cashier said, "Accept it! Save yourself some money. You're pregnant!"

I bought it anyway. The truth finally began to sink in. I cried and cried. I thought back over the years, the pain of losing my dad and my struggle with depression, and it seemed to me that God had brought me through for that moment. But how was I going to tell Barry? I knew he would be over the moon, and I wanted to think of a special way to share the news. I decided to serve the last test strip to him on a plate at dinner. (Don't worry, there was no food on it.)

When he came home that night, I asked if he was ready to eat, but he said he'd had a late lunch and wasn't hungry yet. Aaargh! I waited as long as I could and then said, "We need to eat—it's crucial!"

Barry took his place at the table and waited for his meal. I had the plate behind my back. "What would you most like to be on this plate?"

He thought for a while with that certain look husbands get when they sense that the right answer is important. "Fried chicken and mashed potatoes?" he whispered hopefully.

I laughed and sat the plate in front of him. He stared at it for a moment before the penny dropped.

"Is this yours?" he asked.

"No, I borrowed it from the woman next door," I replied. "Of course it's mine, you silly goose!"

We laughed and cried and laughed and cried. It was such a wonderful surprise. Christian was born on the thirteenth of December

1996. I will never forget the look in Barry's eyes as he held his son for the first time. Wonder, pure wonder!

## CAN YOU LOVE A CHILD TOO MUCH?

What must it have been like for Abraham? He had waited a lifetime to have a child with Sarah, and he finally held him in his arms; the gift, the promise, his son. We know nothing of the years between the birth of Isaac and the day God asked Abraham to offer his son as a sacrifice. Scripture just tells us it was "some time later" when God tested Abraham (Gen. 22:1).

Abraham had listened to his son say his first word, he watched him take his first step, and he saw what a good man he was going to be. He loved this boy deeply. A. W. Tozer, in *The Pursuit of God*, suggests perhaps he loved him too much: "As he watched him grow from babyhood to young manhood, the heart of the old man was knit closer and closer to the life of his son, till at last the relationship bordered on the perilous."

He continues, "It was then that God stepped in to save both father and son from the consequences of an uncleansed love." Scripture tells us, "Then God said, 'Take your son, your only son, Isaac, whom you love, and go to the region of Moriah. Sacrifice him there as a burnt offering on one of the mountains I will tell you about'" (Gen. 22:2).

To me, it has always seemed like such a cruel test. Abraham and Sarah waited for so long for this boy of the promise, and then God asked Abraham to take his own hand and kill his son. He also gave him time for the full impact of what God was telling him to do to sink in: it was a three day trip to Moriah. God spoke to Abraham at night, for we read, "Early the next morning Abraham got up and saddled his donkey. He took with him two of his servants and his son Isaac" (Gen. 22:3).

Can you imagine what that night must have been like, what thoughts must have tormented Abraham?

*How will I bring myself to do it?*
*What will I tell Sarah?*

*What will be my last remembrance of my son as I raise the knife to kill him?*

*What will his eyes say to me?*

But we read that he got up early the next morning and set his heart and mind to do what God had asked of him. He chopped wood for the fire and set off on the longest trip of his life. On the third day, Abraham saw the mountain in the distance and knew that it was the place. "He said to his servants, 'Stay here with the donkey while I and the boy go over there. We will worship and then we will come back to you'" (Gen. 22:5).

I find that one of the most faith-filled statements in all of Scripture: *"We will worship and then we will come back to you."* It wasn't *"I* will worship, and then *I* will come back," but " *We* are going up that mountain together to worship God, and then *we* are coming back!"

Do you see it? Do you see what God had worked in Abraham by then? God had a track record with Abraham. Abraham had blown it over and over again, and yet God had remained faithful. God had proved Himself to Abraham in such profound ways that Abraham knew Isaac was the boy God promised his descendants would come from. If God said it, God would do it! Abraham knew that even if he had to plunge the knife into his son's heart, God could raise him from the dead.

Only God could have prepared Abraham to make that kind of declaration of faith; it is outside my imagination and heart. I have often thought that as I listen to women share their stories with me. I have thought that as I read the notes from my friend Janice. There is a gift of grace and faith that God gives the person in the midst of the trial that He does not give to those who watch. We look on and wonder how it is possible that they still keep on walking; what we can't see is that God is upholding them from within.

"Abraham took the wood for the burnt offering and placed it on his son Isaac, and he himself carried the fire and the knife" (Gen. 22:6). Just as Jesus carried the cross on His back up Golgotha's hill, so, too, Isaac carried the wood that he was to be sacrificed upon. This is a wonderful foreshadowing of the Lamb who was slain to take away the sins of the world. When the catacombs in Rome were discovered and the artwork on the walls studied, the drawings of Abraham and Isaac climbing the mountain and of Abraham with his arm stretched back to slay his son are presented as a representation of God's gift of His Son, and Christ's own sacrifice.

> Isaac spoke up and said to his father Abraham, "Father?"
> "Yes, my son?" Abraham replied.
> "The fire and wood are here," Isaac said, "but where is the lamb for the burnt offering?" Abraham answered, "God himself will provide the lamb for the burnt offering, my son." (Gen. 22:7–8)

They continued up the mountain. At the top they stopped, arranged an altar, and placed the wood on it.

"He bound his son Isaac and laid him on the altar, on top of the wood" (Gen. 22:9). Think about this scene and the physical realities of it. Abraham was well over a hundred years old and Isaac a young man in his prime. Do you think Abraham could have bound him there if Isaac did not willingly lie down? I believe that Isaac trusted his father just as Abraham trusted his God, and they both leaned on God to see what He would do.

> Then he reached out his hand and took the knife to slay his son. But the angel of the LORD called out to him from heaven, "Abraham! Abraham!"
> "Here I am," he replied.
> "Do not lay a hand on the boy," he said. "Do not do anything to him. Now I know that you fear God, because you have not withheld from me your son, your only son." (Gen. 22:10–12)

As Abraham looked up he saw a ram, his horns caught in a bush, a sacrifice provided by God. Can you imagine what it must have been like to cut Isaac free? To hold him and weep on his neck, and to know as deeply as a human being can know this side of eternity is faithful?

Most of us will never have to walk up a mountain this steep, will not be asked to lay our children on a physical altar. But I think there is a message for us here. Tozer implied that God tested Abraham because Isaac had become an idol to his father. It's amazing how quickly something or someone we have received from God as a gift can take the place in our hearts that belongs only to the Giver. I treasure my son, but I know he belongs to the Lord. It is the greatest stewardship given to a man or a woman to nurture and raise a child. It is also the greatest challenge to relinquish him daily to the loving care and sovereign will of our Father.

When I face new trials in my role as a mom, I look back at God's track record with us as a family, and God's faithfulness increases my faith.

## "NEVER" MEANS *NEVER*

"Never will I leave you; never will I forsake you" (Heb. 13:5). We began this chapter with this Scripture. This is God's absolute, rock-solid promise to us. Thomas Lye, the great Puritan preacher, commented on this verse, saying that the Greek here has five negatives. It may rightly be translated, "I will not, not leave thee neither will I not, not forsake thee," as suggested by Jerry Bridges in his book *Trusting God* (p. 197–98).

When we find ourselves in the greatest places of testing, the Lord tells us over and over and over and over and over: *"I will be there!"*

As you look at your life today, with all the pieces that seem to work well and the bits that don't, my prayer is that you will take some time and write out for yourself what God's track record is with you. I hope you will do this rather than concentrate on where you feel you have failed. Consider:

When did you come to faith, or have you yet?
What do you trust about God today that you may not have trusted Him for some time ago?

Can you look back and see God's hand at work now in situations
where you could not see it before?
Do you love God today more than you did a year ago?
Do you believe He loves you?

I believe that God's love for us is overwhelming and His faithfulness unending. Abraham took his beloved son Isaac and was willing to
sacrifice him to his God, knowing Him to be faithful. God, our Father,
took His only Son, let Him carry His cross up a hill and be slaughtered
in our place. Whatever you are facing right now, be it the worst of
times or the best, remember you are loved by a God who spared nothing of Himself to show His faithfulness.

There is a green hill far away, outside a city wall,
Where the dear Lord was crucified, who died to save us all
O dearly, dearly, has He loved, and we must love Him, too,
And trust in His redeeming blood, and try His works to do.
We may not know, we cannot tell, what pains He had to bear;
But we believe it was for us He hung and suffered there.
(Cecil F. Alexander)

Like Abraham and many of the great saints of the faith, I have at
times gone from a mountaintop experience with God to slipping over
the other side in the grip of despair and doubt. So what is the place of
doubt in our walk with God? Is it an attack from the enemy or is it a
gift from God? We'll look at that next.

# CHAPTER 6

# Surprised by Doubt

## When Our Faith Is Shaken

‰

*We walk by faith; He wills it so*
*And marks the path that we should go.*
*And when, at times, our sky is dim,*
*He gently draws us close to Him.*
*And thus by faith till life shall end*
*We'll walk with Him our dearest Friend.*
*Till safe we tread the fields of light*
*Where faith is lost in perfect sight.*
                                        —Fanny Crosby

*Be self-controlled and alert. Your enemy the devil*
*prowls around like a roaring lion looking for someone*
*to devour. Resist him, standing firm in the faith,*
*because you know that your brothers throughout the*
*world are undergoing the same kind of sufferings.*

*And the God of all grace, who called you to his*
*eternal glory in Christ, after you have suffered a little*
*while, will himself restore you and make you strong,*
*firm and steadfast. To him be the power for ever and*
*ever. Amen.*

                                        —1 Peter 5:8–11

*O*ne of my favorite writers and speakers is Dr. Henry Cloud. He and Dr. John Townsend have written many best-selling books, such as *Boundaries, Boundaries for Kids,* and *Boundaries in Marriage.* When I lived in Southern California, Henry and John held Monday evening teaching sessions in a local hotel. It was a very informal atmosphere conducive to asking honest questions. On one particular evening a man said he and his wife were having conflict over bills getting paid on time. "She doesn't trust me to handle this issue without always second-guessing me and questioning me: 'Have you paid the mortgage?' 'Did you make the car payment?' 'What about the phone bill?' It's driving me nuts!"

"Do you pay the bills on time?" Henry asked.

"I do," he said. "I was late once with the bills and we had some interest to pay, but that happened once in three years—hardly a pattern."

Henry addressed the wife. "How did it make you feel when the bills were late, and you had to pay late fees?"

"Well, really I think my husband is making more of an issue of this than it is. I know that he is the head of our home, and I trust God to help him lead with wisdom."

Henry smiled, the husband snorted, and the rest of us giggled a little, partially in embarrassment. Henry then related a story that fit perfectly with the situation and the subject matter of this chapter. This is the gist of it.

One morning a Sunday school teacher asked her class a question. "Children, what is brown, has a bushy tail, and gathers nuts?"

Silence.

"Come on, children, this is not a difficult question. What is brown, has a long bushy tail, and gathers nuts?"

Silence again.

Finally the teacher addressed one of the boys. "Simon, I know you must know. Tell me what is brown, has a bushy tail, and gathers nuts."

Simon replied, "Well, I know the answer is Jesus, but it sure sounds like a squirrel to me!"

How I identify with that story and with the woman in Henry's seminar. We want to say the right thing even if it sounds like a squirrel to us! Within the Christian community we seem to put pressure on ourselves and each other to say the *right* thing rather than the *true* thing. Obviously there are many times when the true thing and the right thing are the same, but when they aren't, we often respond as Simon did.

Ever been there? Ever felt as if the answer you are supposed to come up with as a faithful believer is a million miles away from what your heart is experiencing?

## Don't Let Doubt Win

This is a huge issue for us to address if we want to embrace and live a true and pure faith. I wonder how many people have walked away from a relationship with God because their inner doubts and questions have overwhelmed and isolated them. They live with the fallout of unanswered questions. I met such a woman on a weekend when it seemed as if everything that could go wrong did go wrong on our trip to Shreveport, Louisiana, in 2003.

We started out from Nashville fairly early in the morning; if all had gone as planned, we would have been in Shreveport in the early afternoon. We were supposed to fly through Dallas, but it was experiencing some very bad weather. So, after a three-hour wait in Nashville, our flight was rerouted through St. Louis. By the time we got to our hotel it was almost 11:30. Usually there are one or two bellmen waiting to help with bags, but our hotel had no bellmen—and no luggage carts. Poor Barry had to haul ten large pieces of luggage upstairs by himself as I carried a very sleepy six-year-old boy.

We hadn't had a chance to eat, so after we got Christian settled I looked to see if there was a late-night menu in the hotel. Room service had closed at ten o'clock. Barry said he was starving, so I called Domino's Pizza. We waited for about forty minutes, and there was still no aroma of pepperoni in the air, so I called to check on the order. An extremely harried man told me that he hadn't even started on our order.

"It's a joke!" he said. "It's a bad joke. I'm all by myself. Bill is sick and Frank quit, so I'm all alone."

"I'm so sorry!" I said. "Tell Bill we hope he feels better soon. Just forget the pizza. We're so tired now anyway."

"No, ma'am," he said. "You ordered a pizza, and a pizza you shall have!"

The pizza arrived an hour and twenty minutes later. By that time Christian was asleep, Barry was asleep, and I had a pizza the size of Texas.

The next morning Barry went to the arena to set up, and Christian and I read a few books then left the room for an hour to let the housekeeping staff clean. We decided to go downstairs for lunch but were advised that the restaurant closed at 11:00 AM and wouldn't be open till five that afternoon. Christian had said that he wasn't hungry until he found out that the restaurant was closed—then he informed me that he was starving to death.

I called Barry on his cell phone to advise him that we had landed in a food wasteland, and he should grab something at the arena if he could. He said that he would come back and take Christian to lunch at a local spot a few blocks away. That way I could shower and get over to the arena for my sound check. Once they had headed off, I went back to my room. When I opened the door I saw that the room was clean, but there were no towels. I approached one of the housekeeping staff who was pushing a cart along our floor. "I don't seem to have any towels, ma'am," I said.

"I know, baby," she replied kindly. "We're all out of towels."

"You have no towels?"

"Not a dry one in the house."

"When do you think you'll have some?"

"Could be this afternoon—could be tonight. Lord only knows! They're trying to wash them."

I went back into my room to think about which one of Barry's shirts I could dry myself on. I sat down on the chair by the bed and it promptly collapsed under me, dumping me in a heap on the floor. (I knew I shouldn't have eaten that pizza!) I called Barry and told him that I would have to skip my sound check and find a towel. I went back down to the lobby to ask if they could rustle up just one, even a little one, even a partially used towel or a very fluffy cat! They promised they would send something up.

I was waiting for an elevator back to my room when I heard a woman's voice behind me say, "I suppose you're back with more faith?"

I turned to see if she was talking to me and saw immediately by the intensity of her stare that she was. "Excuse me?" I said.

"Aren't you with that faith group?" she asked.

"I'm with Women of Faith," I replied.

"That's the one I meant. I've been to one of your conferences," she continued.

I got the decided feeling that it had not been a good experience for her. "Are you coming tonight?"

"No, I'm not coming," she said.

"I'd be glad to get you tickets," I said, wondering if cost was an issue for her.

"No, thanks. I used to be very involved in the church, but I don't go anymore."

"Do you mind if I ask why?" I said.

"I used to believe. I used to believe that God loved me, and the church would be there for you when times got rough, but it's a crock. The church is just a building full of people pretending to be okay when they're bleeding to death."

With that she turned and left. I followed her out the front door of the hotel, but she was gone. I felt such an ache as I stared across an empty parking lot. I heard her words, but more than that, I heard her heart. I heard the pain and disappointment, and I wondered what her story was. All I could do was pray for her.

Pray—surely that is the greatest thing we can do for each other, but I think sometimes we need the hug of flesh and blood. I know that at my most painful moments in life I have wanted to see eyes look back at me with compassion and understanding: God present in outstretched arms and listening ears. I wondered if she had any place to take her doubt, her questions, or would that be too risky? How many people have walked away from the church because they didn't dare say out loud what was going on in their hearts?

As believers we find it easy to share what we perceive to be our great moments of faith or insight, but we usually keep our doubts to ourselves. I want us to look together in this chapter at the gift that doubting can be to our spiritual lives. That may sound strange, but I believe that doubts, honestly expressed and wrestled with, produce a faith that is stronger and more intimate than doubts suppressed under the veneer of faith. Perhaps no one experienced that more acutely than the apostle Peter.

## THE ROCK

Most of what we know about Peter comes from the gospel accounts. He was a native of Bethsaida, a village by Lake Tiberias. He was introduced to Jesus by his brother Andrew, who initially was a follower of John the Baptist. We read in John 1:35–41:

> The next day John was there again with two of his disciples. When he saw Jesus passing by, he said, "Look, the Lamb of God!"
>
> When the two disciples heard him say this, they followed Jesus. Turning around, Jesus saw them following and asked, "What do you want?"
>
> They said, "Rabbi" (which means Teacher), "where are you staying?"
>
> "Come," he replied, "and you will see."
>
> So they went and saw where he was staying, and spent that day with him. It was about the tenth hour.

Andrew, Simon Peter's brother, was one of the two who heard what John had said and who had followed Jesus. The first thing Andrew did was to find his brother Simon and tell him, "We have found the Messiah" (that is, the Christ).

At his first encounter with Christ, Peter's name was Simon, but Jesus changed it to Peter. "'You are Simon son of John. You will be called Cephas' (which, when translated, is Peter)" (John 1:42).

Andrew was obviously someone hungry to know spiritual truth and a Jew watching and waiting for Messiah. Although he, according to John's record, was the first to hear and to take his brother to Jesus, Jesus determined that Peter would be the leader of His followers. He is always listed as the first among the disciples and always included in the smaller group that Jesus took with Him in more intimate moments. He was one of the two disciples Jesus entrusted with the preparation of the Last Supper, and one of the three Christ took with Him to the Garden of Gethsemane. Peter illustrates for us all the potential for good, for nobility and courage in a human heart, while modeling also what is flawed and faithless. One of his most remarkable experiences took place in deep water.

## TELL ME TO COME TO YOU

Matthew's gospel has two accounts of large groups of people being fed from nothing more than a person's lunch. After the first, the one we know as the feeding of the five thousand, Jesus sent the disciples on ahead of Him by boat across the Sea of Galilee. He stayed behind to say good-bye to the crowd, which was reluctant to leave, and then He went farther up the mountain to pray. Jesus spent hours alone with His Father that night, preparing perhaps for all that lay ahead, or simply soaking in the joy of His presence.

The disciples were facing a very different experience. That night as they were on the boat, a storm blew up and battered the craft: "The boat was already a considerable distance from land, buffeted by the waves because the wind was against it" (Matt. 14:24).

Matthew Henry, in his commentary on Matthew's gospel (p. 1276; vv. 22–33; 111:1), writes to us out of this passage, "We may have fair weather at the beginning of our voyage, and yet meet with storms before we arrive at the port we are bound for. After a long calm, expect some storm or another."

The men were having a rough time because of the height of the waves and the strength of the wind. Then suddenly they saw something they had never seen before. At first they couldn't make out what it was in the dark. A figure was walking over the waves as if He owned them. I think that must have been a terrifying sight! Some of the men thought it was a ghost, but then they heard Jesus' voice, "Take courage! It is I. Don't be afraid."

Peter responded, "Lord, if it's you . . . tell me to come to you on the water."

"Come," Jesus said (Matt. 14:27–29).

Peter, the one graced with courage, asked Jesus to let him come to Him. I don't think this was theatrics, playing with signs and wonders, for Peter said, "Tell me to come *to you*," not "Wow, teach me how to do that!"

So Peter stepped out of the boat and onto the water with the others looking on in amazement. I think it is a gift to us that after walking on the waves for a moment, Peter looked down and began to sink. I receive two things from that illustration: *Christ is strong*, and *I am weak*. If I keep my eyes on Jesus, I can walk over troubled seas to Him, but it's not because I've perfected Walking on Water 101. It's only because I am looking at Jesus. It was not that Peter had suddenly become a magician but rather that as long as he kept his eyes on Christ, the impossible became possible.

Jesus did not calm the storm that time; He grabbed hold of His friend in the midst of the storm and held him. In my own life, sometimes Jesus has spoken to the stormy circumstances I was in and immediately calmed the sea. Other times, though, even as the storm continued to rage around me, I have cried out to Him and He has reached out and grabbed hold of me.

As you read this passage today, I don't know what you are facing, but I have overwhelming confidence in a God who does and who loves you. One of my passions as we take this journey of looking at faith together is that we see whether Jesus calms the storm or calms us in the storm, His love is the same, and His grace is enough. Peter experienced the love of Christ and the call to press on higher that night. With quick compassion, Jesus reached out immediately and grabbed Peter. The question Christ asked him serves us well in this context: "Why did you doubt?" (Matt. 14:31).

Great question! Not "How could you doubt?" or "I can't believe you doubted!"

Jesus simply asked why. There is no condemnation in that question, but a call to Peter to examine his heart. Jesus wanted him to come to a greater understanding of what it means to walk by faith, not by sight. Asking *why* of ourselves when we doubt is an important step toward faith. Peter could say that he doubted because he took his eyes off Jesus and looked down—a good lesson for the future, for there were many moments of faith and doubt ahead. One of the most remarkable examples of simple faith came through an unlikely vessel.

## I'll Take the Crumbs

Jesus and the disciples had just been through a busy, miraculous few days. They had traveled through the region of Tyre and Sidon when a Canaanite woman asked Jesus to help her daughter, who was demon possessed. Her encounter with Christ is a powerful lesson on the tenacity of faith.

From the land of milk and honey, the land that Abraham almost gave away, came someone who was not a Jew, not one of the chosen race, but she recognized in Jesus the only hope for her tormented child. Initially Jesus seemed reluctant to help her. When she asked for His help, He replied,

"I was sent only to the lost sheep of Israel."

The woman came and knelt before him. "Lord, help me!" she said.

He replied, "It is not right to take the children's bread and toss it to their dogs."

"Yes, Lord," she said, "but even the dogs eat the crumbs that fall from their masters' table."

Then Jesus answered, "Woman, you have great faith! Your request is granted." And her daughter was healed at that very hour. (Matt. 15:24–28)

Twice she received a no from Jesus, but she would not be still. Jesus told her that He had not come to the Gentile nations but to Israel. At that point she could easily have walked away, discouraged and wounded, but she did not. She repeated her plea, "Lord, help me!"

Jesus' next statement would have sent most people running. It sounds cruel and unfeeling, the implication being that she was nothing more than a dog at the table of the chosen. She pressed on still, accepting the analogy and being willing to take the crumbs that would fall to a dog. It seems Jesus was testing her faith to the extreme, and she came shining through. She would not leave until she had tasted mercy from God.

This woman exhibited not only great faith but great humility. So often in the church we are tempted to position ourselves as those who deserve everything that God so graciously showers upon us. I had a conversation with a young woman who told me that she had a picture of a Mercedes Benz convertible on her wall; she believed in faith that God would give it to her. Her explanation to me made perfect sense in her mind: "I'm the daughter of a king. I should look like it!"

How often in our self-serving culture we miss the point that the great riches our Father longs to give us are far more valuable than fancy cars or nice homes. They are the eternal gifts of faith, joy, peace, patience, kindness, purity, perseverance, and hearts that seek His face. The Canaanite woman understood that even crumbs from the hand of Jesus would be more than she could ever ask for.

## IT'S ALL ABOUT HIM

They moved on to the hills by the Sea of Galilee, and a large crowd surrounded them. Word of who Jesus was and what was happening around Him was spreading like wildfire. Some of the most spectacular miracles took place that day. Blind people were healed, those who were lame walked again, the deaf could hear, and those who had been mute from birth found their voices and began to praise God. Can you imagine what it must have been like to be on the hillside that day?

As the day drew to a close, Jesus told His disciples that the people needed to be fed but knew they were reluctant to leave. He asked the disciples to take care of feeding the crowd. Having just watched the impossible happen, the disciples saw only what they did not have.

"Where could we get enough bread in this remote place to feed such a crowd?" (Matt. 15:33).

I have said that very thing many times on a Friday evening as I stand at the back of a packed arena and look out at the crowd. I know that in an hour I will walk onto the stage and face the audience. In my human flesh I think, *Where could we get enough bread in this remote place to feed such a crowd?*

The spiritual hunger seems overwhelming, and I feel so small. I have great empathy for the disciples. Even though they had seen a crowd fed miraculously, it was a new day, a new crowd, a barren location, and there was overwhelming need. So one more time Jesus reminded them that it was not about them and what they *had*—it was about *Him and who He was.*

Again, heaven invaded earth, and from a few loaves and small fish the whole crowd was fed. I have the great honor of seeing that every weekend. I bring the loaves and fishes of my life and offer them to Jesus. He takes them, blesses them, breaks them, and feeds His people. It is a miracle!

## PATSY'S STORY

On our Women of Faith team, no one understands that more than Patsy Clairmont. If you have never read her story, I highly recommend it. In her book, *I Grew up Little, Finding Faith in a Big God,* Patsy chronicles her journey through agoraphobia, crippling fear, three packs of cigarettes a day, and a purse full of tranquilizers! It's just like God that one of her most liberating moments came as she sat paralyzed by fear.

A friend had invited Patsy to attend a women's conference with her. Patsy was virtually housebound and traveled only short distances with her husband, Les, driving. She could not imagine getting in a car and driving several hours to a public event.

Her friend asked her to ask God and her husband before she said yes or no. Patsy was sure that both God and Les would agree that it was impossible, but she felt compelled by both to go. She woke up that morning to a storm. Patsy had a terror of storms and never ventured out in bad weather. She fell on her knees and prayed, "God, what are You doing, letting it storm? I'm doing my best work here. I got up and packed my bag. Can't You help me out here? I don't do storms!"

The thunder continued. The car trip was a nightmare. She was on a freeway (*I don't do freeways*), and she was driving in a strange car (*I don't do strange cars*) to a strange place (*I don't do strange places*) in the midst of a wild storm. By the time she got to the church, all the seats on the lower level were filled and, as Patsy says, "I don't do balconies." As she sat there in a cold sweat, petrified, finding it hard to gasp a breath, one of the speakers took the stage and said, "We are nothing, women, without Jesus Christ."

Then she read the Scripture from Isaiah 55: "Come, all you who are thirsty, come to the waters; and you who have no money, come, buy and eat! Come, buy wine and milk without money and without cost" (v. 1). In her spirit Patsy heard God say to her, "Hope to you little one who sits there so afraid. I see you, and I understand that this life journey is too much for you, but it is not too much for Me."

Each weekend as I watch Patsy bound up the steps to the stage, I look up at the balcony for a moment and wonder if one more petrified woman is about to be transformed by the love and life of Christ.

Patsy shared in 2004 how the story of Elijah has helped and inspired her. But it wasn't Elijah's great moments of faith that brought her comfort and strength—it was his moments of doubt and fear.

Elijah was a man like Peter who had seen God do great things, but like Peter, he was human, flawed, and frail. He had seen God use him to bring life back to a dead child. He had watched as fire fell from heaven to consume a waterlogged sacrifice. But when one woman, Jezebel, sent word that she intended to have him killed, he ran for his life. He told God, "It's enough, I'm done, I can't do this anymore, it's too hard" (see 1 Kings 19).

I find that those who walked with God in the Old Testament seem far more honest than those of us in the church today.

The psalmist David, as I have mentioned previously, was brutally honest with God. The prophets poured out their hearts to God; Job railed against God. Those who were able to bring their doubts and fears, however raw, into the presence of God, and who truly wrestled with their faith, found a faith that could withstand anything. Doubts unexpressed isolate us and drive us from the heart of God. God's heart is big enough to carry whatever burden you are bearing.

Do you doubt that God loves you?

Do you doubt that He cares?

Do you doubt that He even exists and that faith is real?

I encourage you to bring your doubts to Him. He can be trusted with your questions.

In many ways, the apostle Peter was the opposite of Patsy. He was pretty sure that whatever Jesus needed, he was the man for the job. But as he faced the greatest failure of his life, he was about to be transformed too. Peter was about to have his self-confidence decimated, but in the crucible of doubt he would be transformed into a man of faith. We'll look at that next.

# CHAPTER 7

## TRANSFORMED BY CHRIST

### *When Our Faith Is Tested by Fire*

∽

*I'm not ashamed to own my Lord, or to defend His cause;*
*Maintain the honor of His Word, the glory of His cross.*
*At the cross, at the cross where I first saw the light,*
*And the burden of my heart rolled away*
*It was there by faith I received my sight*
*And now I am happy all the day!*

—Isaac Watts

*"But what about you?" he asked. "Who do you say I am?" Simon Peter answered, "You are the Christ, the Son of the living God."*

—Matthew 16:15–16

"I hope you don't mind, but I gave them your name," Cliff said.

"You gave them my name? Good grief, why?" I asked.

"I think you would do a good job," he said with his customary encouragement.

The first time I met Cliff Richard, I was so overwhelmed that I locked myself in the bathroom and stayed there for an hour. Many in America are not familiar with his name, but in Europe, Australia, Africa, and Japan, he is a superstar. You might remember his duet with

Olivia Newton-John, "Suddenly," or his own hits, "We Don't Talk Anymore" and "Devil Woman."

I was introduced to Cliff by my manager, Bill Latham, who also handled Cliff's Christian charity concerts. I opened for him on two British tours, and he produced my album, *War of Love*, my second U.S. release. He became a good friend and an inspiring performer, always professional, prepared, and gracious to those behind the scenes as well as to his fans.

On the day in question, Cliff told me that a producer from BBC television had asked if he was interested in hosting a one hour special on gospel music. Since he wasn't, the producer and I met, and I played him some of my favorite U.S. artists' albums, most he'd never heard of. We taped the special in front of a live audience, liberally spiked with my friends from church for moral support. It was a success, and the powers that be decided to develop a weekly show with yours truly as the host. I loved it! It was called *The Rock Gospel Show*.

It was the first time on British television that we had a Christian program. The show ran for three years. My only frustration was that I was very limited in what I could say about the gospel. If I said too much, it was edited out. My manager came up with a great idea. He decided to book a national tour across Scotland, England, and Wales, which would provide me with a platform to share more about my faith. The tickets went on sale, and soon the tour was sold out. I was very excited about this opportunity and knew that God was going to use it powerfully. I just didn't realize He was going to use it to transform *me*.

## SILENCE

The week before the tour, I developed throat trouble. I was referred to one of London's leading ear, nose, and throat physicians. He ran some tests and took a few x-rays, and then I returned to his office to hear the results. I couldn't believe what he told me. He said that I had nodules on my vocal cords and not only couldn't I sing, I wasn't to talk *for a whole month*. This covered the entire duration of the tour.

I didn't know what to do. My pastor and elders prayed for me. I was sure God would heal me, and that would be one more testimony of His grace and kindness. Instead I got worse. The whole tour was cancelled. I was devastated.

What had I done wrong?

Where had I missed God?

Why didn't God answer my prayers?

A friend of mine asked if I wanted to use her small summer cottage on a beach for a couple of weeks. I gratefully accepted. For ten days I fasted and prayed. I was consumed with questions and self-doubt.

Had the program become too important to me, so God took my voice away?

Had I allowed the opportunity to become an idol?

How had I failed God?

On the last day of my break, I walked along the beach for hours until I found a large rock that looked as if someone had carved it into a cupped hand. I sat down on it with my head in my hands, my silent questions tormenting me. As I sat there, I heard God talk to me. It was not an audible voice but an unmistakable one, and what He said to me was so simple but so profound.

*I have many servants and few friends; many who will do things for Me, few who just want to love Me.*
*Sheila, I don't want your work; I want your heart.*

That encounter transformed me. Many life-altering moments lay ahead, but I knew on that day, sitting on a rock carved out by the sea and the waves, that God loved me because of who He is—not because of what I could do.

## FLAWED BUT FORGIVEN

The apostle Peter found out the same thing. He discovered that Christ knew his flawed heart and wanted to transform him too.

One day Jesus asked his friends what the talk was about Him, who people speculated that He was. They told Him that some people thought he was John the Baptist, Elijah, or one of the other prophets. Jesus turned to look them straight in the eyes and asked this question, "Who do you say I am?" The Greek word for "you" in this context is a corporate word. It was a question Jesus asked of the whole group, but Peter was the one to reply. He said, "You are the Christ, the Son of the living God" (Matt. 16:15–16).

This was a God moment for Peter, a gift from heaven. You might question my crediting Peter's declaration as divinely inspired, as if Peter gets to own only the faithless moments. But Jesus Himself said to Peter, "Blessed are you, Simon son of Jonah, for this was not revealed to you by man, but by my Father in heaven. And I tell you that you are Peter, and on this rock I will build my church, and the gates of Hades will not overcome it" (Matt. 16:17–18).

This revelation from God to Peter must have been one of those moments that he looked back on during the dark night after the Crucifixion. Did Christ's words haunt him that night? *A rock! You'll build Your church on me? The gates of hell crushed You, and I walked away.*

When the disciples began following Jesus initially, they were *hoping* He was the Messiah. They saw the miracles and all the signs that pointed to Old Testament teaching about what Messiah would do; still, they did not fully understand until after the Resurrection that the Crucifixion had to take place. Peter's bold declaration was a moment when heaven filled the heart of an earthly man, but Peter had many troubled days where he had to work out his faith with fear and trembling.

From the moment of Peter's proclamation, Jesus spent more and more time with the inner circle, trying to prepare them for what lay ahead. When He told them that He was going to die, Peter pulled Him aside and rebuked Him privately for saying such a thing. How could Jesus be the Messiah and talk about dying? Messiah was to liberate God's chosen people and reign on the earth—not die on a tree!

Jesus said to Peter, "Get away from me, Satan!" (See Matt. 16:21–23.)

What a shock for Peter. He went from the Rock on which Jesus would build the church to the very devil himself. Jesus heard in Peter's words the enemy of His soul trying to call Him away from the cross—whispers of the temptations in the wilderness when Satan told Jesus He could have everything without the suffering and death on Calvary.

Things were beginning to change for the disciples; the sand was pouring out of the hourglass of Jesus' life. He told His friends, "For whoever wants to save his life will lose it, but whoever loses his life for me will find it." That one statement alone in Matthew 16:25 is one of the most significant keys in wrestling with doubt and living a life of faith. Abraham knew that. God took him to the place where the only thing that mattered to him was doing whatever God asked. My friend Janice is in that crucible. Jesus Himself was soaked in blood and tears in that crucible: "If it is possible, let this cup pass from Me . . . Not My will, but Thine be done."

I, too, have wrestled in that place.

## HELP MY UNBELIEF

I have written in *Living Fearlessly* about a night I spent walking the floors of my home, trying to bargain with God. We had spent part of the day at Christian's pediatrician's office. Our son had seemed listless and pale, so I asked the doctor to check him out. After the nurse took three blood samples, Dr. Ladd told us he would have the lab results in the morning. My heart tightened in my chest as I asked him what the tests were for. He asked me just to wait till the morning, but I pressed for more information. Christian was out of the room, picking out a sticker awarded to brave boys, so Dr. Ladd revealed that he was testing for leukemia. I felt as if a vice had gripped my heart and was squeezing the life out of it.

All that night I walked from room to room in agony. "Please don't let him have leukemia.

"If one of us has to be sick, please give it to me. I beg You, Father: please do this one thing, and I will never ask another thing of You again."

All night I prayed the prayers of the desperate. I threw offers up to heaven and fell on my face and wept.

In the morning we got the news that Christian did not have leukemia—he was anemic. Sometime later I told that story from stage, and a woman met me at my book table that night to tell me she received a different report. "My daughter does have leukemia," she said quietly.

I felt so ashamed of glorying in our good news as another mother was living with such dreadful news. She must have read the expression on my face because she said, "No, Sheila, I didn't tell you that to make you feel bad! I told you that because you need to know that whether you get the answer you pray for or the answer you dread, God's grace will be enough." I marveled at her faith, but I didn't want to trade places with her.

I was Peter before the Resurrection.

I was Abraham, dragging my family to Egypt because it was up to me to save us from starvation.

Did God look down on me and wash His hands of me? No, He never does. Let's follow Peter a little farther down the road.

## A Mountain of Glory Before the Hill of Death

A few days after Jesus predicted His death, He took Peter, James, and John up a high mountain where He was changed before their eyes: "His face shone like the sun, and his clothes became as white as the light. Just then there appeared before them Moses and Elijah, talking with Jesus" (Matt. 17:2–3).

What a moment in human history! Moses, who was not allowed to cross into the promised land, was talking with Christ, the Promise. Elijah, who held the rain back from the earth for three years, was talking to the One who spoke the world into being. But Peter was about to miss the point again.

He said, "If you wish, I will put up three shelters—one for you, one for Moses and one for Elijah" (Matt. 17:4).

In a rare moment, God the Father intervened and rebuked Peter: "While he was still speaking, a bright cloud enveloped them, and a voice from the cloud said, 'This is my Son, whom I love; with him I am well pleased. Listen to him!'" (v. 5).

While Peter was still talking, devising all sorts of plans, God shut him up. That moment was not about Moses or Elijah; it was Jesus' moment. *He* was the one transfigured. I had always assumed all three were brilliant like the sun, but the text does not support that. God's message to Peter was clear: "This is not another prophet. This is My Son."

Sand continued to run out of the hourglass; the clock was ticking for Jesus. He chose two men, Peter and John, to prepare the last meal He would share with His friends. He told them to look for a man carrying a jar of water. That would not be as hard to spot; only the women usually carried water in a jar, and men carried it in leather skins. Jesus had supernatural knowledge of how this final meal would go. He told them that the man would show them to a room that was already prepared for Him, as indeed it was.

It was during this last meal that Jesus gave Peter one of the greatest gifts of all. Peter just didn't recognize it at the time. How could he? Look at what Jesus said: "Simon, Simon, Satan has asked to sift you as wheat. But I have prayed for you, Simon, that your faith may not fail" (Luke 22:31–32).

Do you hear the compassion in Christ's heart for this brave, loyal, passionate but flawed man? Peter, the one who had been the voice for the Twelve, suddenly became the ears to hear what lay ahead for him, for the early church, and for us. When wheat is sifted, grain separates from chaff, the stuff that has no value. Satan's accusation of Peter and the Twelve was that they were nothing more than chaff. Just as with Job, whose story is found in the Old Testament, the enemy asked for permission to shake Peter to prove to God that there was nothing in him but self.

Jesus told Peter that He had prayed for him, that his faith would not fail him. We know from the rest of the story that Peter went on to deny Christ three times. Does this mean that Jesus' prayer for Peter failed? Absolutely not! Peter would fail in the courtyard of Caiaphas the high priest just as you and I will fail God many times in our walks with Him. But ultimately God will prevail, and our faith will stand because Jesus Himself is praying for us.

Are you discouraged at the moment?

Do you feel as if you have failed God one too many times?

"Lord, I believe: help Thou mine unbelief;"
Let me no other master know but Thee.
Thou art the Christian's God, the only King and Chief
Of all who soldiers of the cross would be.
"Lord, I believe," in mercy grant me grace
To know Thee, blessed Savior, more and more;
I can do naught without Thee; Jesus, show Thy face
Unto Thy servant who would Thee adore. (Daniel Howard 1800s)

Let's see the rest of Peter's story before we address that.

## DARKNESS FELL

Peter was wounded and shocked by Christ's statement. "But he replied, 'Lord, I am ready to go with you to prison and to death.' Jesus answered, 'I tell you, Peter, before the rooster crows today, you will deny three times that you know me'" (Luke 22:33–34).

The dialogue continues in the text as Christ talked to His friends, but what was happening in Peter? Christ's piercing gaze of love and truth must have shaken him as much as His words.

"You will deny me not once, but three times, Peter. I'm telling you this in front of all your friends. I called you 'a rock,' for rock you are. I tell you, you will deny Me, for deny Me you will."

After they had shared the bread and wine together, Jesus and the disciples made their way to the Garden of Gethsemane, which lies in the valley between Jerusalem and the Mount of Olives. This was not a new place for Jesus to pray. This olive grove was a place where He had spent many hours alone with His Father. But that night was very different.

Jesus, the Son, was walking into the night of wrestling agony as Abraham had done so many years before over his son. He asked Peter, James, and John to go farther into the garden with Him and pray.

We will never know the depth of the agony as Jesus prayed. We read that His sweat mingled with blood, as if His body were an open wound, and everything in Him cried out for God to remove His cup of wrath. Luke is the only gospel account that tells us that an angel was sent to Jesus to strengthen Him (22:43). I am so grateful we have that piece of the story. Although the cup would not be passed from Jesus, He was strengthened for what was just ahead.

"My Father, if it is not possible for this cup to be taken away unless I drink it, may your will be done" (Matt. 26:42). Isn't it interesting that our perfect world was thrown into chaos as Adam and Eve said, in effect, "Not what You want, God but what we want"? Then Jesus redeemed Adam's fallen race with "Not what I want, but what You want."

Three times He prayed, giving us the example that when we are most afraid, in most danger or sorrow, we should, pray, pray, pray.

When Jesus returned from praying the first time, His three closest friends were asleep. He was so alone. After the third time of tortured prayer, He returned to them again as a large crowd began to move through the garden (Luke 22:47). The sense from Luke's account and the way he usually used the word "crowd" suggests great hostility. Judas had already arranged with the soldiers that because it was nighttime, in the garden he would identify Jesus with a kiss.

I used to think that was strange. Surely they would have known Jesus; but not only was it dark, there were no cameras, no photos then. We are used to being very familiar with the faces of celebrities, but not so in those days. As the soldiers approached Christ to arrest Him, Peter drew his sword and cut off one soldier's ear. John is the only one who identifies the disciple as Peter; the three other writers simply say "one of Jesus' companions" (Matthew) "one of those standing near" (Mark), "one of them" (Luke). But Peter, with the words of Christ still fresh in his mind and heart, reached out in characteristic passion and slashed into the crowd.

I think it must have been shocking when Jesus told him to put the sword down, and then He healed the soldier's ear. He must have thought, *You told me I'd deny You. I try to defend You, and You stop me. I don't understand.*

I think Peter had spoken the truth to Jesus: "Lord, I am ready to go with You to prison and to death." But not like that. That made no sense. I'm sure Peter felt that he would fight to the death, give it all he had, not lie down like a lamb.

*Peter didn't realize that he had been following a Lamb all along.*

Peter followed the crowd at a distance to see where the soldiers were taking Jesus. The teachers of the law and the elders had assembled at the home of Caiaphas, the high priest. Peter slipped into the courtyard and tried to hear what was going on. Hatred was everywhere: Satan prowling around like a lion with the smell of Lamb's blood in the air.

A young servant girl approached Peter and said that she recognized him as someone who had been with Jesus. "But he denied it before them all. 'I don't know what you're talking about,' he said" (Matt. 26:70).

Peter moved away from the brighter light of the fireplace in the courtyard to stand in the shadow of the gateway. But another girl saw him there and repeated the accusation. "He denied it again, with an oath: 'I don't know the man!'" (v. 72).

Peter was sinking fast. The second time he denied Jesus with an oath, as a Jew calling down a curse upon his head if he is lying. Some time passed. Peter's heart must have been bursting in his chest. Another man approached and told him that his accent was a giveaway. The Galilean dialect was very distinct from that of those in Judea. Jesus was born in Bethlehem, close to Jerusalem, but He had grown up in Nazareth, almost sixty miles away. Peter was from a small village farther north in Galilee, and his accent brought the spotlight onto his head. John's gospel tells us that the man who brought the final accusation was one of Caiaphas's servants and a relative of the soldier whose ear Peter cut off.

"Then he began to call down curses on himself and he swore to them, 'I don't know the man!' Immediately a rooster crowed. Then Peter remembered the word Jesus had spoken: 'Before the rooster crows, you will disown me three times.' *And he went outside and wept bitterly*" (Mark 14:74–75, emphasis added).

There are no words to adequately express the bitterness of those tears. Peter had seen through a glass darkly. He thought he knew what was going on, but when it mattered the most, he had failed. We don't know where he went that night or the next day, but Peter must have been a tormented and anguished man.

Did Lucifer visit him that night?

Did demonic voices fill his head and heart?

Did he consider taking Judas's drastic escape?

Nothing made sense to Peter anymore. He didn't know himself, and he didn't know Jesus. But though he thought his life was over, it was really only beginning.

## GOING HOME

After Peter ran into the night, Jesus stood as a condemned man before Pontius Pilate, the Roman governor of Judea. Pilate had no stomach to execute the man. He recognized the smell of a whipped-up frenzy and wanted no part of it. Jesus was taken into the palace courtyard and beaten until His body was unrecognizable. But that was not enough to feed the ravenous crowd. They wanted more: "Crucify Him! Crucify Him!"

Pilate asked for a bowl of water and, symbolically washing his hands of the whole affair, he gave Jesus over to the crowd's lust for death. The guards made Jesus carry His cross along the road known as The Way of Suffering. When they reached the top of Golgotha, they nailed His battered body to a cross.

During the hours that Christ hung there, where was Peter? We don't know, but when the sky at noon turned as dark as midnight, it must have seemed to him as if the world were coming to an end.

Where was Peter when the ground shook, and the graves gave up their dead?

Did he go home to his wife, or did he roam the hills alone like a man possessed?

## Everything Was About to Change

Early in the morning of the third day, Mary Magdalene, Mary, who was James's mother, and Salome went to the tomb to anoint the body of Christ. There they encountered an angel who told them that Jesus was no longer in the tomb. He had risen, and He was going home! The angel said Jesus had gone on to Galilee, and He would meet them there.

Mark recorded the most amazing, life-changing moment for Peter that the other writers omit: the angel added, "But go, tell his disciples and Peter, 'He is going ahead of you into Galilee. There you will see him, just as he told you'" (16:7).

Go tell the other disciples *and Peter!*

There is no way for us to begin to imagine what that must have been like for Peter.

*Jesus is alive? What do you mean, He is alive?*

Would Peter have wondered if he was welcome if the invitation had not been so specific?

"You, too, Peter! Jesus is waiting for you!"

Peter ran to the tomb and went inside. There he saw the strips of linen that had been around Jesus' body and the burial cloth that had been around his head lying separately. The clothes were neatly folded. Christ had no more need of grave clothes.

*I betrayed Messiah.*

*I walked beside Him for three years, and I missed everything He said.*

*He trusted me, and I let Him down.*

*Now He is alive again. What can I say to Him?*

*How can I face Him again?*

## DOUBT TURNED INTO FAITH

I want us to look at one more moment in Peter's life. It didn't take place the first time Peter saw the risen Christ or the second; it happened on familiar territory, as Peter heard a voice across the water.

One evening, Peter and six of the other disciples set out on a boat to fish. They fished all night but caught nothing. Early in the morning they heard someone call out to them, asking if they had caught anything. They couldn't make out who the person was but called back that it had been a fruitless night. The voice suggested that they should throw their nets off the right side of the boat. They did so, and the net filled up with so many fish they couldn't hold them—the net even began to break under the weight! This had happened to them only one other time and with only one person! John looked through the morning mist to the shore and said to Peter, "It's the Lord!"

Peter jumped out of the boat and swam to shore. The others followed in the boat, bringing as much of their catch as they could. After they had all enjoyed breakfast together, Jesus turned to Peter and asked him a pointed question.

"Simon son of John, do you truly love me more than these?"
"Yes, Lord," he said, "you know that I love you."
Jesus said, "Feed my lambs."
Again Jesus said, "Simon son of John, do you truly love me?"
He answered, "Yes, Lord, you know that I love you."
Jesus said, "Take care of my sheep."
The third time he said to him, "Simon son of John, do you love me?"
Peter was hurt because Jesus asked him the third time, "Do you love me?" He said, "Lord, you know all things; you know that I love you."
Jesus said, "Feed my sheep." (John 21:15–17)

The first two times that Peter said, "You *know* I love you," he used a word that translates as head knowledge, intellectual assent, but the third time he changed it to a word that means knowledge gained through experience. Just as Job said to God, "My ears had heard about you, but now my eyes have seen you," so, too, with Peter.

I hear the pain in Peter's words, as if he were saying, "Lord, of all people You know that I love You. You knew I would blow it and that I would walk away. Lord, You know everything, and You know my heart now. I will never be the same. I love You!"

Jesus gave Peter the mission for the rest of his life, an echo back to the Last Supper: "And when you have turned back, strengthen your brothers" (Luke 22:32). In other words, "Feed my lambs." "Take care of my sheep." "Feed my sheep."

Peter was a changed man. After Christ's ascension, he firmly established his role as head of Christ's followers. This was the same Peter and yet a changed Peter. I am so encouraged by this man who struggled with his faith and with fear and doubt. As I said at the beginning of the last chapter, doubts honestly wrestled with can lead to a far more meaningful, personal, vibrant faith.

## QUESTIONS ARE HEALTHY

I have lived long enough to welcome my son's questions. I don't want him to grow up thinking that he has to say the right thing because his mom is a Christian speaker and writer. I know that as he grows, he will wrestle with his faith. I believe it is the only way to grow. God is not offended by our honest questions, for they are a hallmark of true relationship. You may want to point me to the passage in James where doubt is presented as the domain of those who have no solid ground to stand on: "If any of you lacks wisdom, he should ask God, who gives generously to all without finding fault, and it will be given to him. But when he asks, he must believe and not doubt, because he who doubts is like a wave of the sea, blown and tossed by the wind" (1:5–6).

In this context James was addressing those who were facing trials and struggles at every turn. His encouragement was to ask God for wisdom.

"Help me see Your hand in this, Father." "Give me the strength to go through this, Father." "Show me which way to turn." These are the prayers of God's beloved children going through difficult times. James encouraged us to ask God to show us how He is working a bad situation for good.

In my experience, it is possible to struggle with doubt *and* stand by faith on a platform of assurance at the same time. When we were waiting for the results of Christian's blood test, and the threat of leukemia hung over us, I wrestled with God, but I had no doubt that He was right there with me at every moment. We live on this earth with all that is true for us here while holding onto heaven with all we know to be true there. Rubem Alves writes in *Tomorrow's Child*, "Hope is hearing the melody of the future. Faith is to dance to it."

We are still in mortal flesh, but we know where our gaze must be fixed. Early church history records that for the rest of Peter's life, every time he heard a cock crow, he fell to his knees and wept. It is thought most probable that Peter was executed during the reign of the emperor Nero, one of the most violent, vicious persecutors of the early church. When it was time for Peter to be crucified, he asked that they crucify him upside down, as he was not worthy to die in the same way as his Lord. It will be an honor one day to meet Peter, but I don't think he will have anything to talk about apart from Jesus!

Here was a man, a fragile human who wrestled with doubt, was confronted by his own frailty, and yet was so embraced by Christ that His love transformed his life. It is one thing to think that you are doing everything right and that is why God is smiling on you, but it is a life-transforming moment when, just as you realize you have got it all wrong, Christ receives you and entrusts you with the care of His people.

Have you been confronted with your own lack of understanding of what really matters in the kingdom of God? I certainly was as I sat in the palm of that rock on a beach on the south coast of England. Even as the realization struck me, I heard these words from God: "I want to be your friend."

CHAPTER 8

# A Cloud of Witnesses

## *When God's Light Shines Through Us*

∽

*Give me the wings of faith to rise*
*Within the veil, and see*
*The saints above, how great their joys,*
*How bright their glories be.*
*I ask them whence their victory came:*
*They, with united breath,*
*Ascribe their conquest to the Lamb,*
*Their triumph to His death.*

—Isaac Watts

*Let us fix our eyes on Jesus, the author and perfecter*
*of our faith, who for the joy set before him endured*
*the cross, scorning its shame, and sat down at the*
*right hand of the throne of God.*

—Hebrews 12:2

*I* sat at my desk one cold, bleak morning in the fall of 2003. I had just taken Christian to school and reminded him to put his jacket on if the class went out at recess. A strong wind was blowing across the landscape outside, and red, gold, and copper leaves that had been in a pile outside my window the previous evening were now caught up in a mad, swirling tango in the air.

I signed on to the Internet and read that I had thirty-two new e-mails. I automatically deleted those that I knew were unsolicited offers for everything from diet drugs to a note from "Perky Tina," who wanted to meet for drinks! I opened the ones that Martie, my assistant, had forwarded to me. I read a couple of urgent prayer requests and printed them to share with Barry and our Women of Faith team. I was intrigued by a note that Martie had added at the top of her third e-mail: "You might want a cup of coffee before you read this one!"

With coffee in hand, I read the note. I have shortened the note and omitted a couple of details to protect the identity of the sender.

I am so tired of hearing about your perfect life with your perfect son and perfect husband! Just who do you think you are? I was at your conference last weekend and I saw the long line at your book table and you standing there like you think you're a movie star in your cute little suit. I thought this was supposed to be all about Jesus not all about you. Why do you sign autographs anyway? What is that worth? It's just your name on a piece of paper—I think you're a fraud!

I was shocked and hurt by the note, but I have learned in my life to understand that when we strike out at someone else, it's not always about him or her; there may be other things going on. So after another cup of coffee, I e-mailed back and tried to address some of her issues. I told her that Barry and Christian are far from perfect, and they could say the same about me. But because I love them and am proud of them, I love to talk about them. As far as the autograph sessions, I tried to explain that it really has very little to do with a name on a piece of paper; it's more about a desire to connect, to talk, to say thank you or share concerns. I shared one of the passages from the letter to the church in Galatia that is a plumb line for my soul: "Carry each other's burdens, and in this way you will fulfill the law of Christ. If anyone thinks he is something when he is nothing, he deceives himself. Each one should test his own actions" (6:2–4).

I told her that I know that I am nothing without Christ; that any good thing in me is Him. But I went on to share how important these times of connection are for me. When I listen to someone tell me that for years she has been ashamed of taking medication for depression, but God lifted that shame as she listened to me talk, it is one more example to me of the loaves-and-fishes principle; of God taking our little and making it much. I also told her how much encouragement I receive from other women whose stories speak to my heart about God's faithfulness in situations I have not yet faced.

At the end of the note I told her how sorry I was that she had been offended by me and hoped that she might be open to see my heart. I also wrote, "P.S. Glad you liked my suit!" (Luci Swindoll says, "Take everything as a compliment!")

Even though I did not embrace the tone of her letter, I, too, have struggled with the whole autograph thing. If it became clear to me that it was nothing more than handing out a meaningless signature, I would abandon it faster than I abandoned low-rise jeans (one experience of trying those on in a fitting room with a three-way mirror cured me for life!). It's my experience that what we long for at those moments of contact is encouragement, hope, kindness, and connection to one another and to a God who loves us both.

When Paul wrote his first letter to the church in Thessalonica, it is very clear how much he loved them.

> We always thank God for all of you, mentioning you in our prayers. We continually remember before our God and Father your work produced by faith, your labor prompted by love, and your endurance inspired by hope in our Lord Jesus Christ.
>
> For we know, brothers loved by God, that he has chosen you, because our gospel came to you not simply with words, but also with power, with the Holy Spirit and with deep conviction. (1:2–5)

Paul, Timothy, and Silas had spent considerable time there and were deeply encouraged by what they saw God doing in the people. It is clear that Paul attributed the work to God's power and not to himself or his friends: "We always thank *God*."

Paul went on in chapter 2 to describe his heart toward them: "We loved you so much that we were delighted to share with you not only the gospel of God but our lives as well, because you had become so dear to us" (v. 8). I find encouragement and counsel in these words. Paul was so committed to God's best in the congregation in Thessalonica that he was thrilled at the opportunity to share "not only the gospel of God but our lives as well."

Numerous examples exist in both the Old and New Testaments of God's using human examples to demonstrate His power. The culmination of that principle is seen in Hebrews 11, the great *faith* chapter. In preparation for writing about this, I have soaked myself in this passage and delved into many commentaries. I have to tell you I am overwhelmed at the depth of spiritual treasure in that one chapter. From the gates of the Garden of Eden to a father asked to sacrifice his son, the legacy passed on to us is priceless. It's my earnest prayer that what we discover here will unpack for us what it looks like to live by faith. I trust that you will be as blessed as I!

## GOD'S SHOW-AND-TELL

"Now faith is the substance of things hoped for, the evidence of things not seen" (Heb. 11:1 NKJV). This opening definition is a challenge to those of us who like rules and regulations, clear direction and control, and a call to get over ourselves! Faith requires great trust and rock-solid belief in the promises of God. Following Christ is a direct call to let go of our human need to understand everything and trust God.

The writer to the Hebrews made it clear that the list of the faithful that follows his opening comments in chapter 11 are there precisely for that reason; the faithful were sure of what they hoped for and certain of what they did not live to see. The late Dr. J. Oswald Sanders of the Overseas Missionary Fellowship said, "Faith enables the believing soul to treat the future as present and the invisible as seen."

But what we are called to is not blind and stupid adherence to something that makes no sense. The Greek word used for "substance" in Hebrews 11:1 is *hupostasis*. It is a scientific term that means actual, physical evidence as opposed to theory or hypothesis. For example, if I said that if you add red food color to water, you would have red water, that is a theory; but if I demonstrated it to you, I would be showing you the *hupostasis*, the substance of what I believe.

The word used in this passage for "evidence" is *elegchos*. It is a rock-solid legal term. As a longtime fan of the television series *CSI* (Crime Scene Investigation), I have come to understand that evidence overwhelms personal conviction or believability. Gil Grissom, head of the crime lab in Las Vegas, looks for *elegchos*, for as he says, "Evidence does not lie." It is a strong, inclusive term in Greek, meaning the kind of evidence that will be accepted for conviction.

So we begin with an understanding that faith has real substance to it and the kind of evidence that demands personal conviction.

The first two men the writer of Hebrews offers as examples to us are Abel and Enoch. They fall into the category of antediluvians, those who lived before the Flood. (Barry asked me why I had to put that word in and not just say "those who lived before the Flood," so I told him I was just showing off.) Both Abel and Enoch have amazing stories to tell us.

## ABEL: AN ACCEPTABLE SACRIFICE

"By faith Abel offered God a better sacrifice than Cain did. By faith he was commended as a righteous man, when God spoke well of his offerings. And by faith he still speaks, even though he is dead" (Heb. 11:4). I never understood this passage as a child. It seemed so unfair that Abel's offering was acceptable, and Cain's was not. We read in Genesis: "Now Abel kept flocks, and Cain worked the soil. In the course of time Cain brought some of the fruits of the soil as an offering to the LORD. But Abel brought fat portions from some of the firstborn of his flock. The LORD looked with favor on Abel and his offering, but on Cain and his offering he did not look with favor" (4:2–5).

Abel brought what he had, and Cain brought what he had. Why did God consider one better than the other? As I have studied what others have written on this passage, the answer has become more apparent. You may remember that when Adam and Eve, Cain and Abel's parents, rebelled against God and ate fruit from the tree of the knowledge of good and evil, God told them that because of their disobedience, their destiny and that of their offspring had changed. God told the serpent who had tempted Adam and Eve to rebel against Him that for all eternity it would crawl on its belly on the ground and eat dust: a picture of total defeat. We read in Isaiah 65 a description of a new heaven and a new earth, but not for the serpent: "The wolf and the lamb will feed together, and the lion will eat straw like the ox, but dust will be the serpent's food" (v. 25).

God said to Eve that women would experience great pain in delivering children and enmity, or hatred, would exist between her offspring and the serpent's. Again, to the serpent God said, in regard to their respective children, "He will crush your head, and you will strike his heel" (Gen. 3:15).

Genesis 4:1 says Eve "became pregnant and gave birth to Cain. She said, 'With the help of the LORD I have brought forth a man.'" Eve could not have known how many generations would pass through human history before the Christ child would be born. It seems reasonable to imagine that Eve assumed that Cain was the man God had been talking about, and her sin would be dealt with in one generation. Sin is not so easily dealt with.

Another way to look at Eve's statement is to say she spoke with pride, thinking, *Just as God can create, so can I.* Many writers feel that is the more likely interpretation. Whichever way we take her words, we see the beginning of a pattern that will haunt God's people until the return of Christ: a belief that we bring something to the table, that we have something to offer God that we have produced. That deception explains the difference in the offerings the two sons brought.

There are two paths visible here: the dead works of self and the way of the Lamb. Cain brought what he wanted to bring—his work, what he was proud of. Toward the end of the New Testament, the writer Jude referred to Cain in connection with false prophets: "Woe to them! They have taken the way of Cain" (v. 11).

It is always important to read all of Scripture and keep singled-out passages in context with the entire Word of God. In Hebrews we read that "by faith" Abel brought a more acceptable sacrifice (11:4). What does that mean? I believe it means that Abel asked God what He wanted: "What can I bring? What would be an acceptable gift to You?"

Abel had no way of knowing that his simple act of obedience would live on and speak to you and to me today. That brings up another interesting point: those whom the writer of Hebrews counted as among the great faithful cloud of witnesses didn't necessarily see themselves that way. They were walking *by faith,* not by sight.

Abel's offering pointed to the only way we can come to God. Abel brought a lamb to offer to God. I find it wonderful that right from the story of the first family, we are pointed to Christ. Over and over God's Word makes it clear that we have no righteousness of our own, yet how often do you and I try to prove to God that we are worthy? I think back to the years I spent working harder and harder in Christian ministry, trying to win God's approval, missing the whole point that *God's favor rests on those who come with nothing in their hands and the blood of the Lamb on their hearts.* The writer to the Hebrews reminds us of Abel's choice, "And by faith he still speaks, even though he is dead" (11:4).

Abel's legacy to us is simple but profound. His life shows us that God looks for obedience and an absolute confidence in nothing but the shed blood of Christ. It's significant that Cain killed his brother. False religion will always be the enemy of true faith.

Legalism is still trying to squeeze the life out of grace to this day.

## CAIN: GOD'S MERCY STILL AT WORK

For those of us who might feel that God showed no mercy to Cain after he brought a less-acceptable sacrifice, read further in Genesis 4. God gave Cain a chance to redeem himself.

"If you do what is right, will you not be accepted? But if you do not do what is right, sin is crouching at your door; it desires to have you, but you must master it" (v. 7).

God warned Cain and gave him an opportunity to walk away from what was in his heart. Cain refused to humble himself, and instead he brutally murdered his brother. Even after that atrocity, God was willing to show mercy. When God confronted Cain for murdering his brother, He banished Cain from his people. It seems as if at this point Cain "got it"—that what he had done and the subsequent punishment were overwhelming. He told God that he couldn't bear it; he would not survive the punishment. So God again turned toward Cain and gave him what is called a "mark" to defend him. Some think it was a physical mark, others, some sort of a sign.

Interestingly enough, under this protection from God, Cain built a city east of Eden called Nod. Later in Jewish history, this city was one of six that would be chosen in the promised land as a city of refuge for those who had committed manslaughter (Num. 35). It was to be a safe place for those who in a moment of passion had killed and yet deeply regretted their actions. I have always understood the mark of Cain to be a negative thing, a curse—but I see here that it was a mark of God's mercy when Cain had made the worst choices of his life. In others' lives we can see how God sustains us when trouble surrounds us. In Cain we see how God's mercy reaches us when the trouble is within our own hearts.

God's mercy again amazes me. I pray that you are beginning to get a clearer picture of the glorious truth that as you are right now, with all that is true about your life, God loves you. And when you come in the name of Jesus, He bestows grace upon grace, even if you have done what seems to you to be the worst thing imaginable.

## ENOCH, A MAN WHO PLEASED GOD

"By faith Enoch was taken from this life, so that he did not experience death; he could not be found, because God had taken him away. For before he was taken, he was commended as one who pleased God. And without faith it is impossible to please God" (Heb. 11:5–6).

I heard a story on the radio about a mother questioning her child after Sunday school. The mom asked what lesson they learned that day, and the little girl told her it was the story of Enoch. Her mother asked her to retell the story.

> Enoch lived a long time ago and God came by every day and said to him, "Enoch, would you like to take a walk with Me?" And Enoch said, "I'd love to." So they did that every day, just God and Enoch taking a walk together. But one day they had walked and talked for a long time and God said, "Enoch, it's getting really late. We're closer to where I live than where you live now. Would you like to come home with Me?"

I love that interpretation of the story!

Enoch lived right between the Fall and the Flood; he was seven generations away from Adam, and there would be seven more before Noah. Enoch was a descendant of Seth (the child Adam and Eve had after Abel was murdered). Enoch stands alone in a generation that rebelled against God. If you read Genesis 5, you find a long genealogical list of Adam's line. After each name we read these words, "And then he died." But not Enoch; of him it says, "He was no more, because God took him away" (v. 24). Wow!

Enoch's conversion is an interesting one. We read that when he was sixty-five years old, he became father to a boy, Methuselah, whose birth so impacted his life that from then onward, he walked in close relationship with God: "And after he became the father of Methuselah, Enoch walked with God 300 years and had other sons and daughters" (Gen. 5:22).

Was it the miracle of holding his son in his arms that brought him to the heart of God? We don't really know, but Enoch stands as a promise in the middle of a list of the legacy of Adam: "For as in Adam all die, so in Christ all will be made alive" (1 Cor. 15:22).

The writer to the Hebrews says that Enoch "could not be found" and that "before he was taken, he was commended as one who pleased God" (11:5). This implies something interesting. It was clear to everyone around Enoch that he was a godly man. The text doesn't say, however, that everyone liked that about him or listened to him. It does say that when he was gone, they missed him and looked for him.

It's not always easy to live a godly life. We think it's only in our generation that society and culture have become so godless, but it has always been a narrow and difficult road for those who want to follow the heart of God.

Perhaps you feel discouraged. You may live with a husband or wife who is not a believer, or your children may have wandered away from faith. You may work in a place where you are laughed at because you love God and choose not to become involved in some of the activities of others. Remember Enoch, and take heart. Sometimes it's only after we are gone that others realize how much they miss the influence and fragrance of a child of God. We don't always live to see what God is doing, but by faith we rest in the absolute conviction that He is at work, no matter what we see with our human eyes.

We don't know much else about the life of Enoch from the books of Genesis or Hebrews, but Jude (the brother of James) tells us a little more: "Enoch, the seventh from Adam, prophesied about these men: 'See, the Lord is coming with thousands upon thousands of his holy ones to judge everyone, and to convict all the ungodly of all the ungodly acts they have done in the ungodly way, and of all the harsh words ungodly sinners have spoken against him'" (vv. 14–15).

Jude took this quote from a book not included in Scripture: *The Book of Enoch*. This is the oldest of the surviving Jewish writings by someone who actually lived in Bible times. Many Jews and Christians greatly respect this work. Those who question Jude's quotation of a book outside the canon of Scripture should note that there are three occasions in the New Testament when someone quotes other literature or commonly used expressions (Acts 17:28; 1 Cor. 15:33; Titus 1:12). The important thing is that Jude did not call this excerpt Scripture; he simply gave us a glimpse into the life of the man Enoch, which supports the premise that it is not always a popular choice to be a child of God in the presence of evil.

At the conclusion of the story of Enoch in Hebrews 11, we read that "without faith it is impossible to please God" (v. 6). God does not want us to die on the altar of our own efforts to please Him. He wants us to come to Him in simple faith through Christ. Like Enoch, take a walk with God every day. You never know where you might end up!

I'm almost sure that those who make up this great cloud of witnesses had no sense that they were part of such a demonstration of God's grace and faithfulness expressed through human lives. They lived and made choices, not knowing how their lives would encourage us through the centuries.

Enoch was a godly man who left a faithful trail behind, but for the next seven generations godlessness on earth became so perverse that God's patience had reached a limit. Everything was about to change.

CHAPTER 9

# A New Beginning

## *When We Need a Fresh Start*

⤜⤏

*Oh, sinner, turn to Jesus now,*
*No longer make delay;*
*Since Jesus died on Calvary,*
*And opened up the way.*
*The time will come, when Christ will say,*
*Your days on earth are o'er;*
*When you are doomed and cast away,*
*You'll hear My voice no more.*

—A. Roten

*The LORD was grieved that he had made man on the earth, and his heart was filled with pain. So the LORD said, "I will wipe mankind, whom I have created, from the face of the earth—men and animals, and creatures that move along the ground, and birds of the air—for I am grieved that I have made them." But Noah found favor in the eyes of the LORD.*

—Genesis 6:6–8

When Christian turned four, our friend Cindy Wilt gave him a book about Noah's ark. It was a fun book with lots of thick pages for chubby little fingers to turn and cute drawings of animals getting on board two by two. On the same birthday he received a wooden model of the ark and little wooden animals to march on board. That evening he asked if he could float his ark in the bath. I

CHAPTER 9

# A New Beginning

## *When We Need a Fresh Start*

*Oh, sinner, turn to Jesus now,*
*No longer make delay;*
*Since Jesus died on Calvary,*
*And opened up the way.*
*The time will come, when Christ will say,*
*Your days on earth are o'er;*
*When you are doomed and cast away,*
*You'll hear My voice no more.*

—A. Roten

*The LORD was grieved that he had made man on the earth, and his heart was filled with pain. So the LORD said, "I will wipe mankind, whom I have created, from the face of the earth—men and animals, and creatures that move along the ground, and birds of the air—for I am grieved that I have made them." But Noah found favor in the eyes of the LORD.*

—Genesis 6:6–8

When Christian turned four, our friend Cindy Wilt gave him a book about Noah's ark. It was a fun book with lots of thick pages for chubby little fingers to turn and cute drawings of animals getting on board two by two. On the same birthday he received a wooden model of the ark and little wooden animals to march on board. That evening he asked if he could float his ark in the bath. I

118

wasn't sure that it was designed to be used in water, but we thought we would try anyway.

He sat in his bath, and I handed him the boat very carefully as he already had a full load of passengers on board. Immediately it began to sink. He grabbed it, and taking a look inside, he ditched the hippos. "They're too heavy!" he announced.

He tried again, but once more Noah and his crew were heading south. So he abandoned the pigs. "They'll just eat too much, and they smell bad."

Again his craft was sinking. After another unsuccessful try, discarding two lions, two giraffes, and all of Noah's family, he announced, "God's just trying to save too many people!"

The sad truth of Noah's story was that he was the only one on the entire face of the earth who still lived a godly life and acknowledged the presence of God. It's clear from the beginning of Genesis that God's heart is all about love and relationship, but time after time, we as the human race failed Him miserably.

## THE BROKEN HEART OF GOD

I find the passage at the beginning of this chapter extremely sad. Just a few generations from the Garden of Eden, we had broken God's heart. The world had become an increasingly violent and corrupt place where people treated God's grace with contempt.

In Noah's day, men lived very long lives. The length of days was a sign of God's presence with them. Adam lived to be 930 years old, his son Seth lived for 912 years; Seth's son lived to 905. Apart from Enoch, whom God took home when he was just a young man of 365, each descendant lived to be 800 or 900 years of age—until Noah. At that point in human history, God decided that because of the way we wasted our days, He would limit them: "When men began to increase in number on the earth and daughters were born to them, the sons of God saw that the daughters of men were beautiful, and they married any of them they chose. Then the LORD said, 'My Spirit will not contend with man forever, for he is mortal; his days will be a hundred and twenty years'" (Gen. 6:1–3).

Many have wondered who "the sons of God" were. Historically there have been three main views: angels, royalty, or men from the godly line of Seth. Most commentators agree that in this passage the phrase refers to men from the line of Seth. That puts the Flood in context, the sad implication being that even in the line of a man who had walked with God and set a fine example for his family, there was no faithfulness left. Adam and Eve had eaten fruit from the tree of the knowledge of good and evil, but it had not served them or their descendants well. They *knew* right from wrong and consciously chose the wrong path over and over again.

God was so grieved that He regretted ever breathing His life into man. He determined to wash the face of the earth of every trace of every creature that had the breath of life. "So the LORD said, 'I will wipe mankind, whom I have created, from the face of the earth—men and animals, and creatures that move along the ground, and birds of the air—for I am grieved that I have made them'" (Gen. 6:7–8).

In the midst of this dark drama, one solitary player still honored God; one man kept his heart and faith pure and intact: Noah. As God cast His eyes across the earth, He treasured this godly man. We read that Noah "walked with God" (Gen. 6:9). I love that picture. It gives the visual presence to a spiritual reality: Noah wouldn't take a step without God. Isn't it amazing that even though only one man on the whole earth still cared about God, that was enough for God to go to great lengths to spare him, and because of him, his family!

## A TASK THAT TOOK YEARS

I used to imagine that God instructed Noah to build the ark, and a few months later, it rained. But Noah was 480 years old when God spoke to him, and 600 years old when the rains began. Some commentators think that it had never rained before on earth, so the sight of an old man building a boat would have seemed all the more absurd.

The ark was not the kind of rough structure that Christian sank in his bath. It was a very impressive vessel comparable to a small cargo ship today:

> So God said to Noah, "I am going to put an end to all people, for the earth is filled with violence because of them. I am surely going to destroy both them and the earth. So make yourself an ark of cypress wood; make rooms in it and coat it with pitch inside and out. This is how you are to build it: The ark is to be 450 feet long, 75 feet wide and 45 feet high. Make a roof for it and finish the ark to within 18 inches of the top. Put a door in the side of the ark and make lower, middle and upper decks." (Genesis 6:13–16)

Noah must have hired a crew to build his ship. I can only imagine the talk among the men: "What is it we're building again? Oh yes, a ship! That's a great idea—you never know when you're going to need a ship in the desert!" "The old guy's crazy, but at least the work pays our bills."

I wonder if they recognized Noah's devotion. Was he just one more man in the line of Enoch whose light shone brightly, but no one noticed until he was gone? I'm sure those around Noah ridiculed him, but he refused to be discouraged by what he saw with his eyes and trusted God with his heart. He walked by faith and not by sight. Noah's witness was among mankind for 120 years.

## NOAH'S INFLUENCE: HIS LIFE AND HIS WORDS

Peter's second letter makes it clear that Noah did not keep the good news about the graciousness and mercy of God to himself. Until the day that God closed the ark door, Noah called people back to God: "He did not spare the ancient world when he brought the flood on its ungodly people, but protected Noah, a preacher of righteousness, and seven others" (2 Pet. 2:5).

When we read a story such as Noah's in Scripture, all the events take place in a few short verses. But God is patient and merciful, and

He gave those around Noah more than a hundred years to turn away from their violent, destructive behavior. Not a single person humbled himself before God and repented.

What is most remarkable to me about Noah's story is not so much that no one else listened to him, but that each of his three sons did. The boys were all grown and married. I imagine they had their own lives and careers, but they knew their dad, and they knew his heart. They believed that their father heard from God. We are told that the only righteous man left on earth was Noah, so it seems that his sons had walked away from relationship with God. Still, they trusted their father's walk with God. When Noah told his sons that God was going to flood the earth, they believed him.

So, when it was time to get into the ark, Shem, Ham, and Japheth took their wives and followed Noah. Humanity was spared because of one man who trusted God even though everyone else had walked away. His children were spared because this man never stopped believing in the goodness and faithfulness of God.

Do you ever feel discouraged in your family? Are you the only one who still seems to have faith? Does it seem as if your children have walked away from everything you have taught them? Do you seriously question whether your commitment to live a godly life is having any impact at all on those you love?

Noah's story reminds us that our children pay more attention than they appear to at times; his constant walk with God saved his whole family.

## "THE LORD SHUT HIM IN"

Contrary to the popular belief that Noah took only two of every animal into the ark, God instructed him to take seven pairs of every *clean* animal, a male and its mate, and one pair of every *unclean animal,* and seven pairs of every kind of bird. It would seem that while in the ark, Noah and his family would eat only clean meat. God's people lived by a strict dietary code that they maintained even as God was giving the earth a new beginning.

I wonder who was watching as Noah and his sons struggled to get all the animals in and penned off from each other. Did they ridicule Noah as fourteen cows were marched up the ramp and onto the boat? Did they laugh at the sight of birds and beasts, followed by Shem, Ham, and Japheth and their wives? We read, "Then the LORD shut him in" (Gen. 7:16). I wonder if that was the first thing that made those outside start to worry.

"Did you hear that?"

"Did you hear the door slam shut?"

"It seemed to be closed from outside."

"No, it couldn't have been."

"You're getting as crazy as Noah!"

The first day passed, then the second. The crowd moved away and back to life as usual. The people had no idea that *life as usual* was almost over. Three days passed, four, five, and six. But on the seventh day they heard something they had never heard before. "On that day all the springs of the great deep burst forth, and the floodgates of the heavens were opened. And rain fell on the earth forty days and forty nights" (Gen. 7:11–12).

That was no gentle rain. It was a violent outburst that rivaled the violent way those men and women had lived. It must have seemed as if heaven and earth had been ripped in two. Did they run back to the ark then and bang on the door? Did God close the door because He knew that if Noah heard the screams, he would open it? I don't think they had that chance, for the water level rose and rose in torrential fury. The rain fell for forty days and nights, till every man, woman, child, and beast were washed off the face of the earth. Then the rain stopped. The silence must have been as eerie as the roaring water and terrified screams.

Silence.

Not one person left on the face of the earth.

Nothing moved, not a bird, an insect, no laughter in the air—just absolute silence. Across seven continents, all that was visible was a lone boat floating on the surface of the waterlogged earth.

## Considering the Lost

When I watched the movie *The Poseidon Adventure,* I thought of the days of Noah. If you have seen the movie, you will remember that at midnight on New Year's Eve, a ninety-foot tidal wave strikes and capsizes the S.S. *Poseidon.* The Reverend Frank Scott leads nine survivors from the grand ballroom, struggling through steam, fire, and rising water in the upside-down ship to reach the propeller shaft, which is now at the top of the ship. He tries to persuade the others in the ballroom to follow him, but they don't trust his instincts. He knows that only a few moments remain before the glass walls of the ballroom will be compromised, and he begs them to follow. They won't listen. Suddenly another huge, rolling wave hits the ship, breaking the glass of the ballroom windows. Everyone rushes to try and climb an enormous Christmas tree to safety, but it's too late, and they are all lost. It's an agonizing thing for the ten people who made it to safety to watch and listen to the terrified screams of the remaining passengers as they are pulled under the water.

I wonder what it was like for Noah and his family, knowing that friends and coworkers were all lost. It is not a small thing to ignore the God of heaven and earth.

After forty days, the rain stopped and the boat floated on top of the earth. The water level was so great that not one landmark was visible. Even the highest mountain peak on earth was under the water. It stayed that way for 150 days. Six months had passed since Noah's family stepped onto the ark and God closed the door; six months of silence. Was God in mourning for the people He had created to be in relationship with Him who were now gone?

## Land Ho!

Time passed, and the earth was like a pool of tears, but still one voice called out to God from the earth.

But God remembered Noah and all the wild animals and the

livestock that were with him in the ark, and he sent a wind over the earth, and the waters receded. Now the springs of the deep and the floodgates of the heavens had been closed, and the rain had stopped falling from the sky. The water receded steadily from the earth. At the end of the hundred and fifty days the water had gone down, and on the seventeenth day of the seventh month the ark came to rest on the mountains of Ararat. (Genesis 8:1–4)

After ten months the floodwaters began to recede, and the tops of the mountains came into sight. Noah waited for forty more days, then opened the window in the ark and sent out a raven to see of it could find vegetation to rest on. The raven returned. Noah sent out a dove, but it, too, returned, having found nothing to land on. He waited seven more days, then sent the dove out again. The dove returned with an olive leaf!

That must have been quite a day. Noah didn't know what God's plan was. We know the whole story, but all Noah knew was that he was to build the ark and get in with his family. He didn't know if he would ever set foot on earth again. When the dove returned with a fresh, new leaf, Noah must have known that God was giving the earth a new beginning.

When the dove went out a second time, it didn't come back. It had found a place to land; it was then the only creature on earth outside the ark. When God finally told Noah that he could leave the ark, he and his family had been on board for a whole year.

God told Noah that his family should be fruitful and multiply. From three men—Ham, Shem, and Japheth—came every man, woman, and child who then walked on the earth.

What did Noah do upon release from the ark? He built an altar on which he offered burnt sacrifices to God, who then bound Himself to a pact never again to curse the earth on man's account. God then set a rainbow in the sky as a visible guarantee of His promise in this covenant.

Noah is the first man in Scripture to be called "righteous." He earned this title because his faith in God never wavered. He trusted God even though he had no idea what the outcome would be. When I reflect on his life, I am convinced that Noah, like Enoch, must have walked with God many days. It is only when you spend so much time in God's presence that you become convinced of His absolute trustworthiness, no matter what.

So the earth was new, the sky was clear, and once more we had a promise from God of a covenant relationship. It would be lovely to think that evil had been washed away with the floodwaters, but God was not ready to deal with the fallen angel yet. So we multiplied and moved across the earth, and evil and willfulness multiplied too.

## GOD'S PERFECT TIMING

The next hero of faith that the writer to the Hebrews holds up is Abraham. We looked at the life of Abraham in depth in Chapter 5, so I have only a few comments to add here. In Abraham's story I see the great mercy of God: He does not test us beyond what we can bear. And He tests us only when He has built us up in our faith as we have experienced His ways. When Paul wrote his first letter to the church in Corinth, he gave them this very promise: "No temptation has seized you except what is common to man. And God is faithful; he will not let you be tempted beyond what you can bear. But when you are tempted, he will also provide a way out so that you can stand up under it" (1 Cor. 10:13).

I'm sure there are times in your life—there are in mine—when you feel as if God is taking you to the very edge of that promise. Temptation in and of itself is not sin. God allows it in our lives to test our faith; we are responsible only for what we do with the temptation.

Even with temptation, it's my experience, and I believe Abraham's experience, too, that God's justice and standards are always bathed in mercy, and His timing is perfect. He didn't ask Abraham to sacrifice Ishmael even though he was the first boy born. He didn't ask Abraham to offer Isaac when he was just a baby. God waited until He had established faith, character, and hope in Abraham. Only then did He ask him to lay everything down and believe Him to be faithful to His promise, no matter how things looked. I too have experienced that kind of mercy. God took me from a girl who was ruled by fear to a woman who is able, by His grace, to lean on Him and trust Him, no matter what.

## FEAR AND FAITH

Giving birth to a child for the first and only time at forty changed me in many ways. I was never the kind of girl who dreamed of having babies. I was more the girl who wanted to go to India as a missionary. But when Barry and I discovered that we were pregnant, we were overjoyed. I knew that Barry would be an awesome dad, and I knew I would be a good mom because I would choose to be. I just didn't know what Christian would do to my heart.

Whatever boundaries and barriers I had up around my heart before his birth were breached the moment he arrived. The depth of love that I felt for this boy overwhelmed me. Every time he hurt, I hurt too. When the doctor asked me to hold his legs down so he could receive his shots, I would have traded places with him in a heartbeat. When I as a great lover of sleep walked the floor with him all night as he was cutting teeth, I wanted to offer as much comfort to this little lamb as possible.

I have taken as many of his little *diversions* as possible and let other things fall by the wayside when he wants to go digging for worms or paint our faces blue. It has been a daily adventure to walk by his side and coach him on how to deal with life, pain, sin, and his own fragile humanity. What I didn't count on was an old, familiar fear that would invade my relationship with God over my son.

Here's the story. In 2002 CeCe Winans was a guest artist with us at Women of Faith. I love her voice and her spirit. Mary Graham asked CeCe if she would sing the hymn "I Surrender All" at all our conferences that year. It's a wonderful hymn, and when you combine it with the grace and gifting of CeCe, it is powerful. I remember the first time that I heard CeCe sing it—by the end of the hymn, the audience was on its feet (so was the speaker team). It was a holy moment.

> All to Jesus I surrender,
> All to Him I freely give;
> I will ever love and trust Him,
> In His presence daily live.
> I surrender all, I surrender all,
> All to Thee, my blessed Savior,
> I surrender all.
> All to Jesus I surrender,
> Humbly at His feet I bow;
> Worldly pleasures all forsaken;
> Take me, Jesus, take me now.
> —J. W. Van DeVenter

Later that evening as I was lying in bed, trying to get to sleep, I heard God's voice deep in my spirit.

"Do you surrender everything to Me?"

"Yes, Lord: my life, my home, my ministry, everything."

"What about your son?"

"What about Christian?"

I got out of bed and went into the bathroom. I had broken out into a cold sweat, and my heart was pounding. I was shocked at the depth of my response. I found myself back in a very old place, one I hadn't visited in a long time.

## AN OLD FEAR

I gave my life to Christ when I was eleven years old. I loved God and believed He loved me, but I also had an underlying conviction that if I loved something or someone too much, He would take it away. This was not a rational, well-thought-out belief, but rather a residue of losing my father as a child. As I grew up I developed a little wall around my heart to protect myself from being ripped apart inside again. My reasoning was simple: if you don't love anyone too much, it won't destroy you if he or she is taken away. This was not a conscious decision; it was a gut-level survival strategy.

I have a vivid memory of waking up in the middle of the night when I was nine or ten years old, realizing that I needed to go to the bathroom. As I passed my mother's bedroom door, I heard her crying. I didn't go in. I don't really know why. I just had a sense that she needed privacy. So I sat on the other side of the bedroom door and cried too. I didn't know why she was crying, but I assumed it was because she missed my dad.

As a young girl, sitting in my pajamas outside my mom's bedroom door, I made a vow that I would never let myself love too much. I would protect my heart at all costs. As I look back now on my response to my mother's tears, I know that my conclusions about her life were inaccurate. She would tell you that despite the pain and the tears, she has had a very good life, filled with the joy of children and grandchildren, good friends and fellowship. But as a child, I couldn't reason that out for myself. I simply imagined that her heart was irrevocably broken, and that was the risk you took if you ever loved as deeply as she had loved my dad.

I now believe that my response to this perceived insurmountable pain affected many areas of my life. Personally, I was guarded and difficult to really get to know. I had compassion for others in pain but never shared my own. I was always willing to be there if anyone needed me—I just tried to make sure I wasn't needy myself.

## WAIFS AND STRAYS

Mom loves to tell Christian stories of all the characters I dragged home for a meal or a bed for the night because I felt sorry for them. I saw that as my role in life. I remember an occasion that has become family folklore. It took place after our church youth group went on a mission trip to Bognor Regis, in the south of England. We spent much of our time on the streets at this seaside resort talking to young people about Jesus. One boy (I'll call him Will) in particular latched on to me.

Will had been a drug user and had the emaciated look of a heroin addict. He sported a wild Afro hairstyle and smelled very strongly of patchouli oil. I spent a lot of time talking to Will about the love of God and then had the joy of leading him into a personal relationship with Jesus. When it was time for us to return to Scotland, I gave Will my address and phone number. I told him to feel free to contact me if he needed any encouragement.

I didn't hear from him for a while, so I assumed he had found friendship in the church that had hosted our mission. One evening my mom, my sister Frances, my brother Stephen, and I were returning from having dinner at the hotel where Frances was considering having her wedding reception. We didn't even have our coats off before there was a knock on the door. It was our next-door neighbor.

"We have someone in our house who claims to be a friend," she said, rather dubiously. "He says he knows you."

"What's his name?" Mom asked.

"He said his name is Will," she replied.

"We don't know a Will," Mom said.

"I do," I whispered.

Will was escorted in. I will never forget the look on the face of my sweet little Baptist mother as Will the hippy appeared with his Afro hairstyle, his backpack, and his sleeping bag!

Stephen whispered to me, "You are in so much trouble!"

Mom called Roy, the man in our church who had led the mission, and Will spent the night with him as opposed to a widow with three children!

Will was just one of the many waifs and strays I adopted. I seemed to have a built-in radar to detect anyone who was in pain—anyone, that is, apart from me. It seems ironic to me now: if you had asked anyone who knew me then if I was guarded in relationships, he or she would have said no, that I was outgoing and caring. But I was outgoing and caring as long as I was in control of giving. I just didn't want to stand in need of care from anyone else.

## MY OWN DARK NIGHT OF THE SOUL

I remember several bleak moments I experienced as a young woman, when just getting through another day seemed too hard. I have a vivid memory that is as present to me as if it happened last week, but it took place twenty-eight years ago. I shared this at our conferences in 2004. The theme, *Irrepressible Hope,* seemed to call for it, for on that night, I had lost all hope.

It was a cold November evening. I stood on the edge of a bridge and looked at the railway tracks beneath me. I had one thought: *Jump, just jump. It will only take a moment, and it will all be over. There will be no more pain, no more sadness, no more feeling so alone in the world.*

If you had passed by and asked me what was wrong, I would not have been able to tell you. I wasn't a drug addict. I wasn't homeless; I was a seminary student. I didn't want to die. I just didn't want to hurt anymore. I felt as if there were a huge chasm in my heart, a vacant, solitary place.

I loved my family. My mom had always been my biggest cheerleader. I knew that I could have talked to her, but I had nothing tangible to show for my pain. If I had a brain tumor, I would have had something to point to on an x-ray and say, "Do you see that? That's the problem. If you take that away, I will be fine." But heartache doesn't show up on an x-ray.

As I stood on the edge of the bridge that night, I imagined my mom receiving a call from a stranger telling her what I had done. I stepped back from the edge.

Many Christians will be shocked that a believer would even entertain the thought of taking her own life. The sad reality is that many don't just consider it, they follow through. I talk to numerous parents at our conferences whose teenage children have ended their lives. The parents are devastated and plagued with self-doubt.

"Where did we go wrong?"

"Why couldn't she talk to me?"

"What was so bad that he would rather die than face it?"

"Why didn't I know?"

"Why couldn't I save my own child?"

My guarded heart affected every area of my life. Professionally, as a Christian recording artist I never took what I did as seriously as others. While others were perfecting their gifts in rehearsal rooms, I was reading a book. I never checked the charts to see if my record sales were doing well. When I was in the studio recording vocals, I was satisfied with a vocal that I could have improved on. In my mind, if a project didn't do very well, it was because I hadn't given everything that I could have. I couldn't afford to care too much about anything.

I had a very difficult time accepting a compliment and always deflected them with a flip comment. After I had been cohost of *The 700 Club* for two years, one of the cameramen challenged me on this. He said, "I've noticed that any time someone thanks you or compliments you, you brush it off as if you don't care."

"I just don't want to take credit for what God is doing," I replied, somewhat self-righteously.

"Sheila, God has given you gifts and the ability to touch other people's hearts, but you don't seem to enjoy your calling. I wish you could, because I do."

His words stayed with me for a long time, and I recognized truth in them. Part of the call of God in my life has always taken me to public places: television, stages, and platforms. At the time, I had a love-hate relationship with that reality. I loved more than I can put into words being used as the conduit of the love of God to someone else. But I hated the way I felt when the spotlight shone on me; I felt exposed and vulnerable. I didn't want to be so noticed because I didn't like me very much.

## A CROSSROADS

I've written about this before. I used to attribute my feeling no self-worth to being overweight as a young woman or having bad skin, but I think those were only smoke screens for the truth. I think that at a core level I just did not like myself at all, and it would not have mattered what I weighed or what I looked like. I believe now that I saw myself caught in a divine catch-22 situation. Let me try to explain.

I thought I had two options in my life: 1) I could live with full abandon and passion, pour out my life and heart to God and to others, take risks, and give generously of heart and spirit. If I did that, I set myself up for disappointment and loss, for heartache and rejection. 2) I could live cautiously, care about others but not too much, love what I do but not too much, give what I have but hold back some reserve. If I did this I would feel safe; not so alive, but safe.

For years I chose option 2, and I think part of me despised that. As believers we are not called to live safe, small lives. We are called to live as Christ lived, to love as He loves.

*But here is the dilemma: we can live that way only by faith!*

If we do not trust that God is good—that He is in control all the time, no matter what is going on; that whatever we pour out in His name, He will pour back and more into our spirits—we live lesser lives, and God in us hates that. We know intrinsically that we were created for more!

This has been a huge revelation to me, and I want you to get it for your own life. Look at your life as it is right now.

If you are married, chances are, your marriage isn't perfect. I'm pretty confident about that because marriage involves two imperfect people. Barry and I love each other deeply. We have been married for ten years, but I am not everything Barry needs just as he is not everything I need. When I am writing a new book, I drive Barry nuts. He might be sitting watching one of his favorite shows, such as *Trading Spaces,* and I interrupt him with, "Guess what I just discovered about Esau and the antediluvians!" I am so excited, and he is a really good sport about my sermonettes. But every now and again he'll say, "If I have to hear one more thing about Noah and the Flood tonight, I may just self-combust!" Poor man!

But here is what makes our marriage a joy to both of us: we are learning that everything we need we find in God alone, and we get to bring those gifts to one another. If my attitude toward Barry on any given day is based on how he is feeling, we are on very shaky ground. He might be having a great day and feel warm and affectionate, which might motivate me to be sweet and kind. But he might be having a bad day, where he just wants to be left alone for a while. If I am looking to him for how I should respond, I'm setting us both up for disaster.

On the other hand, if I understand that God *always* loves me, *always* watches over me, *always* has grace and mercy for me, *always* offers peace and joy, then I have a full heart that can share warmth and affection with Barry when he is in that place. I can love him enough to give him space when that is what he needs.

Now let me say this: we don't always get it right! Some days the stresses of life pile up, and I give in to my selfish humanity. I think back to that moment just a few weeks ago when we were preparing to bed down in the closet until our apartment was ready, and I lost it over the spider, then accused Barry of overreacting. The old me would have stayed in a defensive mode and mood for some time, feeling as if Barry were mocking me instead of just laughing at my ridiculous statement. Now, because of God's grace and faithfulness to me, I can laugh at myself. I used to have such a fragile core that I felt diminished by any flaw that showed. Now I understand that I am indeed flawed, but I am redeemed and loved by God.

If you and I could meet face-to-face and talk together, I would be able perhaps to communicate the truth more powerfully. But I pray that God's Spirit will do what I cannot do. What I want you to understand is that God has drastically changed and freed me. I don't feel so fractured. In many ways I am more vulnerable, but I am under the covering of the grace of God. I choose now to live within option 1: with full abandon and passion, pouring out my life and heart to God and to others, taking risks, and giving generously of heart and spirit.

I realize that life is full of disappointment and human failure, but

God is immovable, His love and faithfulness are rock-solid, and we can stake our lives on them.

## THE RESIDUE OF CHILDHOOD TRAGEDY

As I've said, I used to associate deep passion with deep pain, and great commitment with great loss. I transferred my fears onto my relationship with God. I imagined that God would test my love for Him by taking away everything I loved, so if I didn't care too much about anything, I would get to keep it. Even as I write this now it seems unreasonable to me, but fear is not a reasonable thing. None of this took place in a conscious dialogue inside my head. It was simply as if the wiring of my soul got crossed, and I lived accordingly.

I wonder if you are able to identify that in your own life.

When tragedy intersects with childhood, it is as if an adult burden has been placed on a child's heart. The child is not able to process the information correctly and comes to wrong but compelling conclusions.

When you look in the mirror, I wonder if you see yourself as you really are or as you were told you were as a child.

When a girl loses her father at an early age, a self-preservation instinct kicks in: *The one who should protect me is gone, so it's up to me.*

It has taken many years for me even to recognize the private vows I made as a child to protect my heart. I am amazed at God's tender mercy with me, gently leading me to a place where I could begin to open my clenched heart and receive His love and protection. Just as God was patient with Abraham and didn't ask him for Isaac until he was in the place to say the confident yes that comes from faith, not the panic-filled yes that comes from fear, He has been patient with me.

## ANSWERING GOD'S QUESTION

I sat in the bathroom that night, reflecting on God's question to my spirit: "What about your son?"

When my heartbeat had returned to normal and my palms had

stopped sweating, I talked to my Father. "Dear Father! Forgive me for the fear that gripped me like an old dreaded ghost. It seems as if part of me still goes back to the place that thinks You'll take everything away from me to see if I love You. I know that You are not like that. I know You are a good, compassionate Father. You have watched over me all the days of my life, and I trust You. I trust You with my son and with my heart. I believe with everything in me that if something ever happens to Christian, You will be with him, You will be with Barry, and You will be with me. So, because of Your love, I relinquish old vows and old ways and choose to live as Your child in Your grace. The greatest joy and the hope I rest in is that forever, we will all be with You. I love You."

I don't write these words lightly. I write them with deep gratitude to God for proving Himself over and over to me and rewriting my internal dialogue. Truly, only God's perfect love casts out fear. Only God could have taken me from a terror of loss to a deep confidence in the God who holds us in the midst of loss. God gives us a new beginning only when His grace is there so we can accept it and walk in it.

That was the experience of Abraham. He went from a faltering and flawed beginning to an abiding trust in God. In many ways, Abraham had not changed. He was still the same man with the same personality traits, likes, and dislikes. But he had walked with God for so long and watched Him do such amazing things that finally he expected God to show up faithfully, whether it was in ways he could anticipate or in unexpected ways. He knew God would always be there.

## Always a Fresh Start

God is a God of new beginnings. Just as He took the earth and washed it clean for Noah and his sons, He took my broken spirit and wounded soul and let me begin again. I find He gives us new beginnings every day.

He gives us a new day to love better, to forgive more, to say that we are sorry, to celebrate the success of another, to be there for a friend who needs us. Our past behaviors do not control us. God makes everything new.

When Abraham took his last breath, he was 175 years old. His sons, Isaac and Ishmael, buried him beside Sarah. His chapter in church history was over, but it continued in the life of his sons.

From Ishmael's line, conflict and chaos continued. If you study Genesis 25, you'll find a detailed account of what happened to both sons after their father's death. Ishmael had many sons of whom we simply read, "They lived in hostility toward all their brothers" (v. 18).

But what of Isaac, the child of the promise? Through the life of Isaac, to his son Jacob and to his son Joseph, it is clear that God is sovereign, He is in control no matter how we might scheme and plot to engineer our own destinies. We'll take a look at Isaac's legacy next.

# CHAPTER 10

# GOD IS IN CONTROL

## *When We Trust in What We Cannot See*

∽

> *I know the Power in Whom I trust,*
> *The arm on which I lean;*
> *He will my Savior ever be*
> *Who has my Savior been.*
> *Therefore in life I'll trust in Thee,*
> *In death I will adore;*
> *And after death will sing Thy praise*
> *When time shall be no more.*
> —Michael Bruce

> *How great you are, O Sovereign LORD! There is no*
> *one like you, and there is no God but you, as we have*
> *heard with our own ears.*
> —2 Samuel 7:22

Faith is believing that no matter how things appear on the surface, God is in control. I think that is both faith's challenge and reward. The challenge is that humanly we want to see with our own eyes what God is doing. We are willing to give an unwavering yes to God if we know His plan and are given the opportunity to sign off on it. But the adventure and reward of faith is that He asks us to trust based on who He is, not on what we can see.

There are many things up in the air for us as a family right now. Where will we live? What school will Christian go to? Should we buy a new home? But God has brought Barry and me to the place of say-ing, "Whatever, Lord! We just want to do whatever You want us to do."

The reward to my heart is that only God could take two opinion-ated, insecure control freaks and work with us until we let go and let Him lead us. For Barry and me, it has been a long and twisted road to this place. It is a long and twisted road for many who are called to walk in God's shadow.

## SON OF THE PROMISE

The theme of this chapter is *God is in control.* Through the lives of Isaac and Rebekah, their sons Esau and Jacob, and Jacob's son Joseph, God's sovereignty shines in the midst of deception and heartache. If you ever feel overwhelmed by everything that's going on in your world and wonder if things are totally out of control, take heart! I think as we trace God's hand through these lives, we will see clearly that no matter what appears to be true, our God is in control.

Isaac married Rebekah when he was forty-four years old. Rebekah, like her mother-in-law, Sarah, had a hard time getting pregnant, so Isaac asked God to help his wife conceive a child. She became pregnant with twin boys. Rebekah experienced a troubled pregnancy. The boys were literally wrestling inside her womb. It was such an extreme prena-tal experience that Rebekah asked God to tell her what was happening to her. Genesis 25:23 says, "The LORD said to her, 'Two nations are in your womb, and two peoples from within you will be separated; one people will be stronger than the other, and the older will serve the younger.'"

When it was time to deliver the boys, the first one to make an appearance had flaming red hair. We read that his whole body was cov-ered with hair. They called him Esau, *Esaw* in Hebrew, meaning "hairy." The next boy came out clinging onto Esau's heel as if to say, "No, me first!" They called him Jacob, *yaaqov* in Hebrew, meaning "supplanter" or "deceiver."

I realize that culturally I am removed from the way names were chosen in those days, but I just can't imagine giving birth to twin boys and calling them Hairy and Supplanter! Is it just me?

As they grew, it became clear that the boys were very different in personality. Esau was a hunter and a woodsman and was very close to his father. Isaac loved to eat wild game, and Esau hunted it down and brought it home to him. Rebekah loved Jacob, who was a quieter boy and stayed close to home. Jacob was also the one who had ambition and would do whatever he had to in order to fulfill his dreams.

As Esau was the firstborn of the twins, he should, by custom, have been the one to receive Isaac's blessing. It was his birthright according to the law of primogeniture. This was an extremely significant position in Isaac's culture. It brought responsibility and blessing. The firstborn had precedence over all the other children in the family. The role was even more significant to Isaac's sons; the one who received the blessing would stand in line with Abraham and Isaac, and through him, the line would continue to Messiah. He would also be the family priest and receive a double portion as an inheritance.

For example, if Isaac died leaving ten thousand sheep, over six thousand of them would belong to Esau and only three thousand to Jacob, even though they were born just moments apart.

But God had told Rebekah things were going to reverse in her family, and the elder would serve the younger. He didn't tell her why. He just said that it would be so. God does not always tell us why His plans are different from our plans; He just asks us to trust Him.

## THE POWER BEHIND THE PLAN

I imagine that Rebekah told Isaac what God revealed to her. As the boys grew, and he favored Esau, God's plan was not what Isaac wanted. But God is sovereign, and even when we try to change His plans, God's perfect will prevails.

I take great comfort in that as a mother. Barry and I will do our best to love Christian well and teach him how to honor God. But we will make mistakes. We named him Christian after the central character in John Bunyan's book *A Pilgrim's Progress*. I want Christian to understand as he grows that life is a journey with many hills and valleys, heartaches and joys, good choices and poor choices, and that God will be with him in all of those moments.

That matters to me because it's easy to second-guess yourself as a parent: *Is this the right school? Are we in the right church? Are we giving our children the best counsel? Should they be living with their heads stuck in a Gameboy player?*

I make it a daily discipline to relinquish my hold on Christian and his future. I want God's best for him, not what seems best to me. Isaac wanted to honor the law of primogeniture and give his blessing to the firstborn son, who was closest to his heart. I understand that, but Isaac would soon understand that God's plans are never thwarted.

The path to realizing that indeed our heavenly Father knows best, and being able to rest in that with confidence and joy, is often a painful one. Isaac, Esau, and Jacob were about to discover that.

## THE DRAMA UNFOLDS

Esau stood in line to inherit great blessing and honor from his father, Isaac. But it became clear as the story unfolded that he was not a man with sufficient integrity and wisdom to value such a calling; in fact, he was willing to squander it to satisfy his immediate needs. Jacob wanted what Esau took so lightly, and he determined to wrestle it away from him. I'm sure he had no idea just how easy that was going to be.

Esau came in from the fields one day and announced that he was hungry. Jacob had cooked a stew, and Esau asked if he could have some. Jacob saw this as his moment and told him he would sell it to him for his birthright. Esau's immediate need and appetite overwhelmed any thoughts about the future. He said to Jacob, in effect, "Sure, you can have it. What good would it do me anyway, if I starve to death?"

His response was very casual, so Jacob made Esau swear an oath that for the meal, he was selling his blessing. Esau agreed, and it was sealed. It's hard to imagine that he would give up so much for so little. God was about to bless Isaac financially, and Esau threw his birthright away for a meal.

Esau's life became a chronicle of bad choices. When he turned forty he married two Hittite women who made Isaac and Rebekah's lives miserable. We don't know much about the circumstances, but it seems sad that after Isaac and Rebekah begged God to bless them with children, they should have so much heartache.

I find everything that we struggle with today wrapped into the pages of God's story. When we bring children into the world, we are full of hopes and dreams for them. We pray that they will be healthy and strong; that they will have good hearts turned toward God. We trust that they will grow up and make good decisions. But often our children become sidetracked or make poor life choices. I find it fascinating that you can have two children raised in the same environment, with the same parents, and yet they grow up to take very different paths in life. So it was with Jacob and Esau.

## THE BLESSING

Isaac realized that he was getting old, his sight was failing, and it was time to bestow the blessing on his firstborn son. He called Esau to himself and asked him to go out hunting, bring back his favorite meat, and then he would bless him. Rebekah overheard the conversation and determined that Jacob would be the one Isaac blessed. Mother and son concocted a plan. Rebekah asked Jacob to bring two prime young goats from Isaac's herds, and she fixed the meal for Isaac.

Human appetite plays quite a role in the tragedy of this family. Esau casually gave away his birthright for a meal, and Isaac insisted on one before he would give his blessing. If he had blessed Esau when he called him in, Jacob wouldn't have had the time to deceive him.

Jacob was concerned about the deception. He knew that his father was almost blind but worried that Isaac might touch his skin and realize it was not rough and hairy like Esau's. Then Jacob would have received a curse, not a blessing. Blessing and cursing in biblical days were not what we think of in our culture. We pray God's blessing on each other and avoid cursing out of a desire not to grieve the Holy Spirit. In Isaac's time, blessing or cursing determined the path a man's life would take.

Rebekah was committed to ensuring that Jacob received the blessing, knowing that once Isaac had given it, he could not take it back. Jacob took the goats to his mother, and she made Isaac's favorite meal. She covered Jacob's hands and his neck with the skin of one of the goats. Timing was everything. At any moment Esau could return from the hunt, so, with the plan in place, Jacob went to his father.

Isaac was initially suspicious. He asked how Jacob was able to go out hunting, find the right animal, bring it back, and have it prepared so quickly. Jacob replied that God led him to the right place, and he was able to make the kill quickly. All the time Jacob's heart must have been pounding in his chest. He knew that if Esau suddenly came back, the plan would fall apart. Isaac was still not sure that he was indeed Esau, so he asked Jacob to come close so that he could touch him. He said, "The voice is Jacob's, but the hands are Esau's. Are you really my son Esau?"

Jacob said, "I am."

Isaac drew Jacob down to kiss him. Smelling the fields and the livestock from the goatskin, he was finally convinced, and he gave his blessing to Jacob. It was a magnificent blessing: "May God give you of heaven's dew and of earth's richness—an abundance of grain and new wine. May nations serve you and peoples bow down to you. Be lord over your brothers, and may the sons of your mother bow down to you. May those who curse you be cursed and those who bless you be blessed" (Gen. 27:28–29).

Isaac had attempted to thwart God's declared plan and award the birthright to his firstborn, but it had failed. God is faithful to Himself. He is faithful to His Word. He works through tired old men and protective mothers. He works through lazy sons and deceptive sons, faithless daughters and fear-filled daughters. The story of Jacob and Esau is a clear declaration of the sovereignty of God. We may interfere with it but never change it.

I find it interesting that this old man who tried to change the plan of God is the same man who climbed the mountain with his father, Abraham. He watched his own father obey God, even if it meant sacrificing the son that God had promised him. Sadly, having seen God work powerfully in one situation is no guarantee that we will respond with the same faith next time.

Just as Jacob left the room, Esau appeared and, realizing what had happened, was overwhelmed with grief and rage. Did he forget that he had sold his birthright? Or was he happy to go back on the deal behind Jacob's back? Had he planned on doing this all along—tricking Jacob into believing that he had purchased the birthright, then keeping it—knowing that he was his father's favorite?

Whatever was in Esau's heart when he took an oath with his brother made little difference then, because it was too late. In that moment Esau realized what he had done and begged his father to bestow a blessing on him too. Isaac could not bestow on Esau anything he had given to Jacob. Things were set in place just as God intended.

It is interesting to note that the very deception that Jacob played out on his father would revisit him in the very near future. So often the seeds that we plant in another's life bear fruit in our own. But for now, Jacob had wrestled the blessing away from Esau.

Esau was devastated. He knew that his father's health was failing, so he determined that after Isaac died he would murder Jacob. Rebekah found out about his plan and told Jacob to run to save his life. She sent him to find his uncle Laban, her brother, who would welcome him and keep him safe.

## DECEIVED BY LABAN

Laban did welcome his nephew into his home and family. Jacob settled in and began working with Laban's livestock. After he had worked for Laban for a month, his uncle said, "Just because you're family doesn't mean you should work for nothing. I want to pay you." But Jacob was not as interested in money as he was in Laban's youngest daughter, Rachel. He asked if he could marry her. Laban told him that if he would work for him for seven years, at the end of that time he could marry her. Jacob agreed. The one whose path of betrayal took him to his uncle's door was about to be deceived himself.

Rachel had an older sister, Leah. She was heartbroken that Jacob fell in love with Rachel and not with her. By rights she should have been married first, as was the custom then. Her father had great sympathy for his firstborn daughter. He knew that she did not have Rachel's beauty, and it would be more difficult for her to find true love and protection. He determined that he would intervene on her behalf.

In an attempt to honor Leah, Laban tricked Jacob. The wedding day arrived. It was a day that Jacob had awaited for seven long years. He stood beside his bride but was not allowed to see beneath the veil that covered her face during the ceremony. The following morning when Jacob lifted the veil to gaze into the eyes of the woman he loved, he discovered that he had not married Rachel; he had just married Leah!

This time, Jacob was devastated. He had worked so long to win Rachel's hand. The depth of his love for Rachel, found in Genesis 29:20, is crystal clear:

"So Jacob served seven years to get Rachel, but they seemed like only a few days to him because of his love for her."

I wonder if the betrayal seemed all the more bitter because he, too, had been the perpetrator of deception with his brother Esau. Jacob asked his uncle how he could do such a thing. Laban told Jacob that he had tricked him out of compassion for Leah. She was not a beautiful woman, and he didn't want to humiliate her in their community where tradition dictated the eldest daughter would marry first. He said that if Jacob would treat Leah with kindness as his wife, and allow her to celebrate her bridal week, then he could marry Rachel, too, at the end of that time. The only other commitment was that he had to promise to work for him for seven more years.

## LOVELESS LEAH

Rachel and Jacob seem to have one of the great love stories of the Old Testament, for Jacob agreed. He honored his week with Leah and then married his beloved Rachel. It was clear to everyone that Jacob didn't love Leah and was passionately in love with Rachel. My heart goes out to Leah. What must that have been like, to look into the eyes of her husband, and all she could see was tolerance? The ensuing conversations and arguments must have been humiliating. It's a hard thing for a woman to realize that she is not the stuff that men's dreams are made of.

It was clear to God, too, that Leah was in a heartbreaking situation. We read that He had compassion on Leah, and she became pregnant and gave birth to Jacob's first son. She hoped that the birth of their son would turn Jacob's heart toward her, but it didn't. She gave Jacob four sons, then she stopped having children.

Rachel was desperate to conceive, but she couldn't, so she asked Jacob to sleep with her maid, Bilhah. Rachel could count the children as her own. Bilhah gave birth to two boys. When Leah saw what was taking place, she asked Jacob to sleep with her maid, who also gave birth to two boys. (Does it seem to you as if the women are dealing with all the emotional agony and heartache here, while Jacob just sits there, welcoming one more woman into his tent?) Leah begged God for more children and was able to give birth to two more sons and a daughter, Dinah, Jacob's only girl.

Their home was full of the sound of laughter and children's voices, but Rachel's heart was broken. She had to live with the harsh reality that Jacob had ten sons and a daughter, but not one child was from her own womb. So we read that God had compassion on Rachel and opened her womb. She gave birth to a son. They named him Joseph.

## JACOB THE WRESTLER

Finally Jacob and Rachel had their child. The one who had fought all of his life for what he wanted held the fruit in his arms. But Jacob was a different man by then. He had wrestled all his life. He wrestled from the moment his hands were formed enough to grasp his brother in the womb. Then he wrestled the blessing away from Esau. He even wrestled with his father-in-law for his wife and found himself the victim of deceit.

In Genesis 32 we read that he wrestled with a Man all night long. When dawn broke, the Man told him to let Him go, but Jacob refused to release his grasp until the Man blessed him. Perhaps by this point in Jacob's life he knew that no matter what he gained through all the scheming in the world, it meant little without the blessing of God on his life. It was at this moment that God changed his name from Jacob to Israel. He went from "deceiver" and "supplanter" to "he who struggles with God and with man and has overcome." From his line, from the great nation of Israel, Messiah would come. Jacob had literally wrestled with God, face-to-face and survived. "So Jacob called the place Peniel, saying, 'It is because I saw God face to face, and yet my life was spared.'" (Gen. 32:30).

It's wonderful to trace the clear path of God's faithfulness and blessing from His promise to Abraham that his descendants would be greater than the stars in the sky, and He would bless all nations through him, to Isaac and then to Jacob, who was now called Israel. We don't always see God's plans take place before our eyes. We don't always get to be the ones who marvel at the fulfillment of them all, but the writer to the Hebrews reminds us that this great cloud of witnesses remained faithful and calls us to live like them.

I remember a wonderful gentleman in my home church in Ayr, Scotland, who prayed for his wife for many years without seeing her come to faith. He never gave up; he believed right up to his last breath on earth that he would be reunited with her one day in heaven. When he died, she still had not accepted Christ, but I remember the joy in my mother's voice the day she called to tell me that we had a new sister in the kingdom. This wonderful, faithful husband didn't live to see his wife surrender to Christ on earth, but he will get to worship at the feet of the Lamb with her in heaven.

Some of you have prayed for a loved one for years, and the temptation is to become discouraged and lose hope. But as long as you have breath, you have hope. God answers prayer in His time and in His way.

## The Golden Boy

Hebrews 11 lists many names of those who are commended for their faithfulness to God, but for our purposes here I want to look at just one more: Joseph, Jacob and Rachel's son. He was the eleventh child born to Jacob. God's faithfulness to this boy was easier for him to see in retrospect than when he was living through long years of betrayal, false accusations, and imprisonment.

That may be true for you too. Again, we don't always get to see God's plan when we are living in it. At times it can even seem as if everything has gone wrong, and God has abandoned us. Joseph's whole story is found in Genesis chapters 37–50, but a few highlights will speak to us as we consider the fact that God is in control, no matter what circumstances say. You may find yourself in a situation right now where it looks as if God has forgotten all about you, but Joseph's story calls us to hold on by faith.

First, we have to go back to his father. Israel was not a difficult man to read. Just as his love for Rachel was obvious to all, so was his partiality to Joseph. This was the child he had waited for from his beloved wife. If there had been talk shows in those days, they would have had a field day with this family of eleven children, four mothers, and one father! Jacob spoiled Joseph, and in doing so, he set him apart from his brothers. Just as jealousy ate at the women in Jacob's life, his children were about to experience what it's like when a parent favors one child over all the rest.

Genesis 37:3–4 tells us, "Now Israel loved Joseph more than any of his other sons, because he had been born to him in his old age; and he made a richly ornamented robe for him. When his brothers saw that their father loved him more than any of them, they hated him and could not speak a kind word to him."

The gift of his *coat of many colors,* an ornate robe, was simply one more strike against Joseph. It said to the other brothers that this boy was special, different, more loved by their father than they were. It will become clear as we see Joseph's life unfold that he had a very specific call on his life from God, that God would use Joseph's gifts to deliver him from a devastating place. But as a young man he lacked the wisdom to use his gifts wisely.

For example, God gave Joseph a dream, which he shared with his brothers. "He said to them, 'Listen to this dream I had: We were binding sheaves of grain out in the field when suddenly my sheaf rose and stood upright, while your sheaves gathered around mine and bowed down to it'" (Gen. 37:6–7). The brothers were furious at the implication that they would one day bow to Joseph. This was their little brother!

## Youth Is No Excuse for Bad Behavior

I think there is a lesson for us here. Joseph was just a boy, but I can think of another teenager to whom God gave a remarkable gift. Rather than wave it in the others' faces, she held it close to her heart. Do you remember what Mary, the mother of Jesus, did just after the shepherds had visited her newborn baby, God's Son? We find it in Luke's gospel: "So they hurried off and found Mary and Joseph, and the baby, who was lying in the manger. When they had seen him, they spread the word concerning what had been told them about this child, and all who heard it were amazed at what the shepherds said to them. But Mary treasured up all these things and *pondered them in her heart*" (2:16–19, emphasis added).

Mary could have said to the shepherds, "This is the Son of God. God chose *me* to give birth to Messiah!" Mary felt no need to prove to anyone what God had said to her. She let God tell the story in His way and in His time.

After the angel of the Lord told her she would have a son, and He would be the Son of God, she responded this way: "'I am the Lord's servant,' Mary answered. 'May it be to me as you have said'" (Luke 1:38). Mary sensed deep within her spirit that she was walking on holy ground. The goodness of God in choosing her overwhelmed her, and she sang, "My soul glorifies the Lord and my spirit rejoices in God my Savior, for he has been mindful of the humble state of his servant. From now on all generations will call me blessed, for the Mighty One has done great things for me—holy is his name" (Luke 1:46–49).

I wish that I had exhibited more of Mary's grace and humility throughout my life. The whole concept of *pondering* was alien to me. It is only in recent years that I have begun to understand the wisdom of saying less and listening more. The boy Joseph, too, failed to exhibit Mary's humility or wisdom at that point in his life. He felt a need to tell his brothers that he was destined for great things, which just made them hate him all the more.

Our gifts can be a blessing or a curse. If Joseph had *pondered* his dream in his heart, it might have caused him to walk humbly with his brothers. He had no way of knowing the path that would lead him to the place where they would indeed bow before him, or how devastating it would be.

Do you feel a call on your life?

Do you know that God is going to use your life in a powerful way to impact the lives of others?

I urge you to follow the example of a teenage girl who kept the greatest news in the world just between her and God until the time was right. Everything that God revealed to her she treasured and meditated upon. God is in control.

## THE PATH OF SUFFERING

Joseph had a second dream. This time the sun, moon, and eleven stars bowed down to him. Joseph told his father about the dream, and Israel was angry with his son for suggesting that there would ever be a day when he, Rachel, and all his sons would bow before him. There would come such a day, but Joseph would have been through betrayal and heartache by then, and he would be a changed man. Often the path that leads us to the place where God can use us most effectively is a path of suffering.

I remember as a young woman making bold declarations to the Lord: "Lord, I want to be used by You, whatever it takes." "Take my life, Lord, and mold me to be more like Jesus." "Father, I long to be a conduit of Your love."

I sincerely meant those prayers. I just had no idea that the path that led to being made more like Christ could be such a dark and lonely place, or that molding requires so much pressure and heat.

I meet so many women through our conferences who feel that they are called into some type of public ministry.

"I've got some great news for you!" one said.

I looked up at the woman who was next in line at my book table. "I love great news," I said.

"I'm going to be doing what you're doing."

"That's wonderful," I said. "It's one of the greatest privileges in life to watch God touch other people through you. Do you have a sense of what you might be sharing?"

"No, I don't have a clue, but as I watched you up there on that stage, God spoke to me and said, 'You're going to be up there soon.' I'm just waiting to see what my story will be."

I prayed for her before she left. Only God knows the plans He has for us or the path that will take us to the place where we have a story to tell. At times, if we knew the path that would take us to a public platform, we would run in the other direction. I'm sure that Joseph had no idea what lay just around the corner for him.

## BETRAYAL

One day his father asked him to go and check on his brothers, who were out with the flocks near Shechem. Perhaps Israel hoped that if Joseph appeared caring to his brothers, it might begin to breach the chasm between them. Instead it set in motion a murderous plot.

When the brothers saw Joseph in the distance, they decided to get rid of him. One suggested they kill him and throw him in an abandoned well. But Reuben, Jacob's firstborn, stopped them and proposed that instead of having his blood on their hands, they should simply throw him in the well and leave him there. "Then we'll see what comes of his dreams" (Gen. 37:20). So they attacked their little brother, stripped him of the robe their father gave him, and threw him into the empty well.

They had no way of knowing that they had just put in place the first piece of the puzzle that would lead to the fulfillment of those dreams. Joseph had no way of knowing that either. The brothers sold him to a passing slave caravan headed for Egypt for twenty shekels of silver.

It is hard to ignore the foreshadowing of the life of Christ that is evident in Joseph's story. Perhaps of all the stories in the Old Testament, no other has so many similar elements.

Joseph was about to be humiliated and then exalted, just as Christ was humiliated on the cross and then exalted to the right hand of the Father. Joseph was sold for a bag of silver and betrayed by one he trusted, as was Jesus. For the betrayal and brutality that he suffered, Joseph did not seek revenge but offered forgiveness and mercy to those who had offended him. Christ cried out from the cross, "Father, forgive them for they know not what they do."

Joseph was sold into slavery in Egypt to Potiphar, captain of Pharaoh's guard. God blessed him there and blessed Potiphar through him. Joseph worked hard and was eventually put in charge of the entire household. He had grown into a very handsome man, and Potiphar's wife tried to seduce him. Joseph resisted, saying that he could never dishonor God or her husband, who had been so kind to him. So she told her husband that he had attempted to rape her. Potiphar had Joseph thrown into the king's jail. Once more he was betrayed, and this time it was because he refused to sin.

Where was God when this was happening? Did God see what was taking place in the life of this honorable young man? The interesting thing to note about this passage is that we read, "But while Joseph was there in the prison, the LORD was with him; he showed him kindness and granted him favor in the eyes of the prison warden" (Gen. 39:20–21).

It is clear in the life of Joseph that even when the worst things imaginable happened, God was with him. God didn't stop those things from happening, but He was with Joseph. Years later Joseph discovered that the path to the place of honor that God had prepared for him, as Pharaoh's right-hand man, prime minister of Egypt, led through those prison walls. He had no way of knowing that the years he spent in jail, during which time he learned to speak Egyptian, were getting him ready for God to raise him up.

## You Raise Me Up

Pharaoh had a troubling dream, and no one could interpret it for him. His cupbearer, who had spent time in prison with Joseph, told Pharaoh that Joseph could interpret dreams. Pharaoh sent for him. He told Joseph his dream and asked him if he could tell him what it meant. Joseph said that he couldn't do that, but God could. As God revealed the meaning to Joseph, he interpreted the dream for Pharaoh.

The dream had serious national and international consequences. Joseph told him that he had seven years to get ready for a famine that would follow seven years of rich supply. If they didn't prepare and store food, the entire nation would be destroyed. Pharaoh appointed Joseph to be the one in charge of all the preparations. I have heard some question why a man as powerful as Pharaoh would give this huge responsibility to someone he had just taken out of prison. It is very clear why from the text: "Pharaoh asked them, 'Can we find anyone like this man, one in whom is the spirit of God?'" (Gen. 41:38).

It was obvious to the Egyptian ruler that Joseph was a man full of the Spirit of God. He gave Joseph his signet ring, dressed him in fine robes, and put him in charge of all of Egypt.

## A Dream Fulfilled

After seven prosperous years, a severe famine plagued the whole earth. The only country that had food was Egypt, so people came from all the surrounding countries to buy grain. Joseph was in charge of the distribution.

One day a group of ten men bowed before him and asked that they might buy grain. Joseph looked down at the tops of their heads as they knelt at his feet, and he recognized them. He was looking down on his brothers. Can you imagine what that must have been like? Did his mind travel back to his boyhood home and a day when he told his brothers about a certain dream? Now there they were, at his feet, at his mercy, the ones who had tried to destroy his life.

It was not time for Joseph to reveal his identity to them. He questioned them about their father and discovered that Rachel, his mother, had given birth to another son and then had died. Joseph said that one of them, Simeon, had to stay in Egypt while the others returned to their father with food. When they came back with the youngest brother, Benjamin, they would all be free to return home.

When the brothers told Israel everything that had taken place, he was horrified. He had lost Joseph, beloved son of Rachel; he could not lose Benjamin too. Finally, when all the food was gone, he relented, and the brothers returned to Egypt with Benjamin. When Joseph saw his brother, the only other child of Jacob and Rachel, he left the room and wept.

Joseph's heart was very tender. He was a good man. He wept because of all the evil and the lies and the sin that destroy people's lives. He needed to know if his brothers had changed, if they had learned anything from what they had done to him. He asked his servants to hide his silver cup in Benjamin's sack of grain, and the next morning he sent the brothers home. They hadn't traveled very far when Joseph's men stopped them and accused them of stealing the silver cup. The brothers were horrified and protested their innocence. They opened all their sacks, and the cup was found in Benjamin's, so they were all escorted back to Egypt. Joseph told them that they were free to go, but Benjamin had to remain as his slave.

## THE TRUTH AT LAST

That was the moment of truth. Would they turn and run, abandoning the boy as they had Joseph? Judah spoke up and offered himself in Benjamin's place. He told Joseph a story that Joseph was very familiar with: their father had two sons by Rachel. The first son was gone, and the grief had almost destroyed their father. They could not return without the other son. Joseph had heard all he needed to hear. He asked all the servants to leave, and he told his brothers who he was.

Scripture says that Joseph wept so loudly that everyone in his house heard the noise, and the story got back to Pharaoh. All the years of disappointment and heartache, betrayal and abandonment, poured out of his body like an excised wound. Soon he was reunited with his father, Jacob. Even though Jacob was an old man by then, they had seventeen years together before he died.

When Jacob's bones were carried back to Canaan to be buried, though, Joseph's brothers were afraid that since their father was gone, Joseph might punish them for their betrayal. Joseph's proclamation to them is one of the most glorious in the Old Testament, and it is a lifeline to us today: "Don't be afraid. Am I in the place of God? You intended to harm me, but God intended it for good to accomplish what is now being done, the saving of many lives" (Gen. 50:19–20).

What a statement of faith! Joseph acknowledged everything that was true. He told his brothers that he knew their intentions, but God was bigger than any of their plans. Joseph was able to trace the hand of God through the cruelty of his brothers and the betrayal of others.

*True forgiveness and grace is possible only when we believe, deep as the marrow in our bones, that God is in control.*

Can you imagine how it will liberate us, if we are able by God's grace to access this truth? We are not victims tossed around on the whims or evil intent of others. By faith we stand on the firm foundation that we are daughters of the King of kings. He watches over us and will not allow anything to happen to us that has not first passed through His hands of mercy.

It is interesting to note that the one thing the writer to the Hebrews said about Joseph has nothing to do with his betrayal by his brothers, Potiphar's wife's false accusation of rape, or the years he spent in an Egyptian prison. The one thing that he picked out of Joseph's life is this: "By faith Joseph, when his end was near, spoke about the exodus of the Israelites from Egypt and gave instructions about his bones" (11:22).

What a strange incident to pick out of this man's life! And yet it is a profound statement. Now I see that it was an absolute gift of faith. As Joseph, by God's gifting, looked down the years to the time when God's people would be held captive in Egypt, waiting for deliverance, he entrusted his bones, his memorial, to them to remind them that no matter how things may appear, *God is in control.*

# CHAPTER II

## MY HEROES

### When We Are Changed by the Faithfulness of Others

*Faith of our fathers! living still*
*In spite of dungeon, fire, and sword;*
*O how our hearts beat high with joy*
*Whene'er we hear that glorious word!*
*Faith of our fathers! holy faith!*
*We will be true to thee till death!*
—Frederick Faber

*But if you suffer for doing good and you endure it,*
*this is commendable before God. To this you were*
*called, because Christ suffered for you, leaving you an*
*example, that you should follow in his steps.*
—1 Peter 2:20–21

When I was a little girl, I wanted to be Snow White. I didn't want to be Cinderella. As far as I could tell, she was either wearing rags or ball gowns, and that didn't seem like a very practical wardrobe to me. She was also very blonde and, believe it or not, when I was growing up I had jet-black hair. (I asked Jack, my hairstylist, recently if I should go back to my natural color, and he informed me that I no longer have a natural color!)

Snow White had dark hair and seven cool little guys to be her buddies; even Grumpy wasn't grumpy around her. (I guess I was always destined to have a son. The only problem is, he just refuses to wear the pointed hat and curly toed shoes!) I loved her kindness and her sense of humor and that she could whistle.

When Christian was five years old, he was invited to a dress-up party for Harvest Festival, a party that friends of ours were having instead of Halloween. He wasn't sure what kind of costume he wanted. First he was going to be the Tin Man from the Wizard of Oz, then Batman, then a Power Ranger or a Star-Trooper. He finally settled on the Tin Man. I got his costume together and found silver face paint and silver spray paint to cover his rain boots. When the big night arrived and he was fully in costume, he looked fantastic. He loved his outfit until he looked in the mirror—then big tears began to make tracks down his silver face.

"What's wrong, sweetie?" I asked.

"I look ridiculous!" he said.

"You look perfect."

"I look like a big silver stick!"

"You look like the Tin Man."

"I don't want to be the Tin Man," he whispered.

By then Barry was at the bathroom door, telling us that we were running late.

"We'll be right there," I said. "We just have to change."

"Why do you have to change? He looks great."

"He looks like a big silver stick!" I said.

Barry rolled his eyes and told us to hurry up.

"Okay, Christian," I said. "I have a backup costume. Do you want to be Sully from *Monsters, Inc.*?"

"Cool!" he said. "How did you get that costume?"

"I ordered it after the movie, when you said that if you were ever invited to a dress-up party, that's who you wanted to be. I forgot all about it! It's in the closet with my costume."

"Your costume?"

"Yes, my costume."

"I think the party is just for kids, Mom."

I ignored his comment, and we quickly transformed him from a big silver stick to a big blue monster. "Go and join Dad," I said. "Tell him I'll be there in a minute."

When I walked into the living room, I thought Barry and Christian were going to explode. They laughed and laughed as I politely ignored them.

"Are you really going like that?" Barry asked.

I just whistled!

I caused a lot of laughter that night, dressed up as my childhood heroine, Snow White, but I didn't mind a bit. I had a wonderful time and was careful to avoid any apples. (Fairy-tale humor.)

As I have grown, my heroes have changed. I have looked to those whose lives have left a bright and faithful path for those of us who are coming behind. That's the kind of woman I want to be. I want to be an encouragement to others; fortunately, as Patsy Clairmont says, "God uses cracked pots!"

## ONE VERY WHOLE "POT"

One of the joys of being the cohost of *The 700 Club* for five years was the opportunity to meet and interview some inspiring women. It was during this time that I discovered a few new heroes—but none more so than Ruth Graham.

I grew up with a great love and appreciation for Dr. Billy Graham. The Billy Graham Association's British office was opened the year I was born, 1956, after very successful crusades in London and Glasgow in 1954 and 1955. When I was in my twenties, I was invited to sing at one of the crusades in England. I was overwhelmed by the invitation and more than a little nervous.

The entire crusade team makes up an amazing and very original group! Cliff Barrows has been the music and program director from the first crusade in Los Angeles in 1949. He is one of the most gracious, godly men I have ever had the joy of meeting. George Beverly Shea has been the official crusade soloist through all the years. He is such a fine gentleman, with a voice that fills stadiums with power and passion. He also has a great sense of humor. I think he recognized that I was nervous that first time; as we were heading toward the stage he asked if I needed to use the rest room. I told him that I was fine, but he said, "Just go for me. Think of it as an insurance policy!"

Earlier in the evening, everyone gathered in the prayer room and Dr. Graham came in and prayed with us. He is a very striking man, tall and tanned, with a very firm handshake! I remember wondering who the elegant lady was who stood off to one side. As we were leaving the room, I was introduced to her. This was Ruth Graham. Ruth is very slender and elegant with a warm smile and kind eyes that sparkle when she talks. I remember thinking that first time, *I bet she can whistle.*

(Now, I realize that whistling is not a spiritual gift, but to me it signifies a woman or girl who doesn't take herself too seriously and yet is not embarrassed to make herself heard either.)

Over the years I have had the great privilege of getting to know Ruth better and calling her "friend." After a couple of years at *The 700 Club,* Pat Robertson gave me my own show, which aired daily right after the club. It was called *Heart to Heart with Sheila Walsh.* I had more time and freedom to go in-depth with a guest in that format—thirty minutes with one visitor per show. I asked my producer what she thought of doing a week of shows with the Graham family, and she was excited about the idea.

## MY FAIRY GODMOTHER

Ruth was kind enough to invite us to come and film at the house, Little Piney Cove in Montreat, North Carolina, and asked if I would like to spend the night after the tapings. It was an evening I will never forget. We filmed two shows with Ruth and two with Gigi, one of her daughters, who is a writer. I had already taped a show with Dr. Graham on his seventieth birthday, so we had that one in the can. When the filming was over, the crew left and Ruth invited me to join her in the garden.

Their home sits high up on a mountain. It is peaceful and beautiful. We sat and talked for a while until I became aware of a small aircraft that appeared to be flying too low. It was getting closer and closer to us and losing altitude as it approached. Ruth seemed unperturbed, but I was getting more nervous with every passing second. Finally I stood up and said, "I think that plane's in trouble. It looks like it's going to hit us!"

Ruth just smiled and said, "Oh, don't worry about that. That's just Franklin buzzing his mother!" The thought of Franklin Graham dive-bombing his mother, and her remaining perfectly calm, confirmed my first impression. I know she whistles!

That evening after dinner, we sat by the fire and talked about books and writing. Ruth encouraged me to read the works of those who have left their mark through the centuries, and not only contemporary authors. That piece of advice alone enriches my life to this day. We talked about what it means to live by faith. Ruth shared the tears she had shed over Franklin before he came to Christ. She told me that one of the passages of Scripture that transformed how she prayed is: "Do not be anxious about anything, but in everything, by prayer and petition, with thanksgiving, present your requests to God. And the peace of God, which transcends all understanding, will guard your hearts and your minds in Christ Jesus" (Phil. 4:6–7).

She said, "I knew how to pray and I knew how to petition God, but I had forgotten that we are called to do it *with thanksgiving*. I began to thank God for Franklin, for what He was doing in his life. It was as if a huge burden was taken away from me." Ruth helped me understand that praying with thanksgiving shifts the focus from our desperate need to a firm gaze at our Father, who is more than able to keep us.

Too soon it was time to turn in for the night. "Let me show you your room," Ruth said. I followed her into a lovely bedroom with a beautiful white embroidered blanket on the bed. It was turned down, the way all beds are in fairy tales.

"May I bring you some tea?" she asked.

"I would love that," I said.

I thanked her and got into my pajamas. A few moments later she knocked on the door and brought me a cup of tea in a delicate china cup. She sat on the end of the bed and read to me. I thought I had died and gone to heaven!

Do you ever have those moments when you look at your life and think, *How did this happen?* There I was, a girl from a small town on the west coast of Scotland, who grew up with no dad and very little money, who couldn't travel more than five miles in a car as a child because it made her throw up. There I was, tucked up in bed in Billy and Ruth Graham's house with a cup of tea and a story! La-di-da! God is good!

## A FRIEND INDEED

I was touched by Ruth's kindness on that trip, but it was her act of grace and mercy to me the following year that has left a lasting impact on the woman I am today. In the fall of 1992, the depression that had sung its mournful song in my heart for so many years was about to overwhelm me and drown out any notes of hope. I felt that I had failed God and everyone else who knew and loved me. I was filled with shame that I couldn't pull myself together. I wrote in my journal, "Lord, I am lost. I have no strength left, I am so afraid. It's not that I don't know what to do; it's that I know there is nothing I can do. I am so tired. I am so alone."

I have written in my book, *Honestly*, about the time that I spent in a psychiatric hospital diagnosed with severe clinical depression. When I was discharged from the hospital in Washington, I returned to Virginia Beach to decide what to do next. I knew that I couldn't go on as I had been. Pat Robertson was very gracious. He was willing to find a less stressful place for me at the Christian Broadcasting Network until I was well again. But I didn't think that was the right thing; I decided not to work for a time.

I was living in a little apartment on the beach, and every morning I took my Bible and walked for miles along the shoreline. During those days I found such comfort in the psalms of God's people reflecting on their days of wandering. For example, Psalm 107:

> Give thanks to the LORD, for he is good;
>> his love endures forever.
> Let the redeemed of the LORD say this—
>> those he redeemed from the hand of the foe,
> those he gathered from the lands, from east and west,
>> from north and south.
> Some wandered in desert wastelands,
>> finding no way to a city where they could settle.
> They were hungry and thirsty,
>> and their lives ebbed away.
> Then they cried out to the LORD in their trouble,
>> and he delivered them from their distress.
> He led them by a straight way
>> to a city where they could settle.
> Let them give thanks to the LORD for his unfailing love
>> and his wonderful deeds for men,
> for he satisfies the thirsty
>> and fills the hungry with good things. (vv. 1–9)

As I continued to journal, a habit I adopted in the hospital, it became clear that I was afraid of people. I was afraid of not being loved, of being rejected because I was weak, of being thrown away. I know now that the loss of my father as a young child left a well of want in me, a need to be approved. I never wanted to rock the boat or be controversial in any way. Now that was all blown out of the water, and every time I went to the drugstore to fill my prescription for my anti-depression medication, I prayed that no one would recognize me.

One day I was sitting on the beach with a cup of coffee, my Bible, and the mail that I had just picked up. I read Psalm 107 again: "Some wandered in desert wastelands, finding no way to a city where they could settle" (v. 4). I prayed, "That's how I feel, Lord. I feel as if

I am in a desert, a dry and merciless place with no place for my heart to settle."

I looked at my mail and saw a padded envelope that had a familiar address at the top—Ruth Graham's. My heart sank. I thought, *Oh no, Ruth has heard what happened. She is writing to tell me she is shocked by what's going on. Perhaps she wishes that she had not allowed me to film the shows with her.*

I opened the envelope and took out a little book, *Streams in the Desert*. Ruth had inscribed the most loving, tender words of grace and mercy and assured me of her prayers during that time. I soaked the book with my tears. I wept and wept for a long time. It seemed too good to be true. It wasn't just that Ruth had reached out with love and grace, but I heard a stronger voice speaking through this dear friend. I heard God say,

> *I am with you;*
> *I will never leave you;*
> *There are streams of My love in this desert place;*
> *Do not be afraid.*

I would love to share that same grace with you at this moment.

Are you discouraged by your life?

Do you feel as if you have failed God one too many times?

Do you feel that if the whole truth about you were known, you would be rejected?

Let me remind you that our Father in heaven knows everything about you and loves you more than I could ever put into words. Perhaps the words of Psalm 118 will speak to your heart as they do to mine: "In my anguish I cried to the LORD, and he answered by setting me free. The LORD is with me; I will not be afraid. What can man do to me? The LORD is with me; he is my helper" (Ps. 118:5–7).

Sometime after my release from the hospital, I wrote a book about my journey called *Honestly*, and Ruth was gracious enough to write an endorsement: "I have loved Sheila Walsh since we first met in England. That she has suffered so will be a shock to many. And yet, through it, because of it, God will use her to minister to many hurting Christians."

It meant the world to me that Ruth would stand side by side with me in such a broken place. It is not difficult to find those who will acknowledge you when things are going well and you appear successful. What a gift it is when someone you love and respect publicly hugs you when you are down.

I have watched Ruth over the years as she takes a quiet place behind her husband, loving to mingle with the crowd during a crusade rather than sit on the platform. She is soft-spoken and unassuming, but she is a giant to me. She has fought the good fight of faith on her knees in prayer, and her life is a conduit of the life and love of God.

Three other women have left quite an imprint on my soul. I would like to tell you a little bit about them. They are my heroes. Their lives have been and continue to be a legacy of faith to me.

## NEY BAILEY: TO BE CONTINUED, FOREVER

As a culture, we have become accustomed to turning the page of a magazine and seeing one more celebrity with a milk moustache and the familiar question, "Got milk?" Let me let you into a little Women of Faith backstage lingo. If any of us are stuck on an issue of faith or can't locate a Scripture, we are very likely to use the phrase "Get Ney!"

Ney Bailey is a remarkable woman, and I am grateful to say she is my friend. I first met Ney through Mary Graham, as they have shared a home for many years. My first impression of Ney was of a very gentle, kind woman with a musical laugh. Over the years, as our friendship has grown, I find those words inadequate to describe the kind of woman she is. She has a steely faith, she is compellingly compassionate, she loves to laugh and she has a heart hungry for God. My whole family adores her.

Before I met Ney, she was an adoption caseworker in her home state of Louisiana. In 1961 she joined the staff of Campus Crusade for Christ, founded by Dr. Bill Bright. Dr. Bright wrote of Ney, "Everywhere Ney goes she gives two things: her heart and her knowledge of God's Word." Some time ago Ney wrote a book, *Faith Is Not a*

*Feeling*. I was fascinated to read her story. I have known her as only a rock-solid believer, so I found it very helpful to track her steps.

What prompted the book was a tragic event that took place in 1976. Ney and thirty-four other women in leadership roles in Campus Crusade had met for a retreat at a ranch in the Big Thompson Canyon near Loveland, Colorado. The weather was lovely, and they went horseback riding and swimming. It was a time to rest and relax in the company of women with a similar heart and vision.

That night, after a home-cooked meal, they sat together in a barn and shared stories of all God was doing in their lives. One of Ney's friends, Carol Rhoad, related an experience she had that very afternoon. She had taken a nap and missed the hayride, so she took a walk around the ranch. One of the ranch workers commented that although they were used to having groups stay, they had never encountered a group so peaceful and full of joy. Carol took it as an opportunity to tell him about her relationship with Christ and how he could know Jesus personally too. Carol had no way of knowing that it was the last opportunity she would have on this earth to tell someone else about Jesus. The retreat that began as a gift was about to turn into a nightmare.

As the group relaxed over coffee, they heard an announcement: "This is the police. Evacuate immediately! The river is rising! A flood is coming this way!"

The women quickly left the barn and piled into eight cars, but since they were unfamiliar with the area, they had no idea where higher ground was. It was dark, and in the confusion they spread out in different directions. The decisions made in the next few moments cost some their lives. Ney followed a police car, but when he continued to yell at them to get to higher ground, Ney and her party abandoned their vehicle and scrambled up the hillside. Eight women reached the top, but they had no idea where the rest of their group was. As they sat huddled together, they began to pray and to sing. "Father, we adore You. We lay our lives before You."

Ney writes, "As we prayed, a peace settled over us as God calmed our fears and comforted our hearts. In the depth of our hearts, we laid our lives before Him."

After some time, the police signaled that it was safe to return to their cars and drive on to Fort Collins, and from there back to their homes on the Colorado State campus. As far as Ney knew, that night when she finally laid her head on her pillow, all had safely been evacuated. The next morning she discovered that many of the women were missing.

As the day progressed, they learned that seven of their friends had perished in the river when two cars were swept off a bridge. Ney struggled with intense grief, but she chose to align her broken heart with Paul's words in his first letter to the church in Thessalonica: "Be joyful always; pray continually; give thanks in all circumstances, for this is God's will for you in Christ Jesus" (5:16–18). She began to thank God that she had known those women and for the time she had been able to spend with each one. She wrote, "God's Word is truer than how I feel."

As I write this chapter I've just returned from spending the day with Ney, Mary, and Luci in Frisco, Texas, where they live. It was my forty-eighth birthday and Barry, Christian, and I had a little birthday party with our dear friends. As we talked over brunch in one of our favorite restaurants, our conversation turned, as it always does, to the faithfulness and goodness of God. Each one of these women I love dearly has made choices in the most painful places in life that affect who they are today. They have chosen to believe that no matter how they may feel, or what circumstances seem to say, God is good and loving all the time. I am a richer woman because of their choices. Every time Ney and I say good-bye, we always say, "To be continued, forever."

## CORRIE TEN BOOM AND BARRACKS 28

When I graduated from London Bible College in 1977, I joined European Youth For Christ as a musician and evangelist. I was part of a band called Oasis, made up of singers and musicians from Holland, Germany, Italy, and Scotland. We traveled all over Europe singing in schools, churches, coffee shops, and theaters, but we were based in Holland.

Holland is an interesting country. It is totally flat. If you put two bricks by the side of the road, you would have the first Dutch mountain range. I loved living there. Canals were everywhere, and everyone owned a bicycle. They drank strong coffee, ate tons of licorice with salt on it, and they put mayonnaise on their French fries!

Our base was in a small town close to the city of Utrecht. Every now and then we had the opportunity to go into Amsterdam, the capitol of the Netherlands. My favorite thing to do was attend a Bible study on a ship docked there called *The Ark*. It was on one of those weekend visits that I discovered that Amsterdam was fairly close to Haarlem, the birthplace of Corrie ten Boom. I had read Corrie's book *The Hiding Place* when I was a student at LBC and was anxious to visit the place where this amazing woman was born. It was just a fifteen-minute train ride from Amsterdam to that lovely old Dutch city, and one Saturday I bought a ticket and went by myself. I stood outside the clock shop above which Corrie and her family had lived. I marveled that in such a simple place God prepared a woman of great faith—that would take her through the unthinkable horrors of two prisons and a Nazi death camp.

The Ten Boom family were devoted Christians, and their home was always an open house for anyone in need. During World War II, the Ten Boom home became a hiding place for fugitives and anyone pursued by the Nazis. By protecting those people, Casper ten Boom and his daughters, Corrie and Betsie, risked their lives. They hid Jews, students who refused to cooperate with the Nazis, and members of the Dutch underground resistance movement.

The Corrie Ten Boom Foundation estimates that during 1943–1944, six or seven people lived illegally in that home: four Jews and two or three members of the Dutch underground. Additional refugees were also welcome to stay with the family for a few hours or a few days, until another safe house could be located for them. Corrie began to organize the care and shelter of those in trouble. This single woman became a ringleader within the network of the Haarlem underground. She searched for courageous Dutch families who took in refugees, and she spent much of her time caring for those people once they were in hiding. Through this selfless love, the Ten Boom family and their friends saved the lives of an estimated eight hundred Jews and protected many Dutch underground workers.

But on February 28, 1944, a neighbor betrayed the family. Nazi secret police set a trap and waited throughout the day, arresting everyone who came to the house. By evening, they had taken more than twenty people into custody! Casper, Corrie, and Betsie were all arrested. Although the secret police systematically searched the house, they could not find what they were really looking for: the Jews in the house were safely hidden behind a false wall in Corrie's bedroom. In this secret room were two Jewish men, two Jewish women, and two members of the Dutch underground. The house remained under surveillance, but the resistance workers were able to liberate all six of them two days later.

Even though the Nazis were unable to find the Jewish refugees, they discovered underground materials and extra ration cards, and on those charges they imprisoned the Ten Boom family. Corrie's father, Casper, died after only ten days in Scheveningen Prison. When Casper was asked if he knew he could die for helping Jews, he replied, "It would be an honor to give my life for God's ancient people" (http://www.corrietenboom.com/history.htm).

Corrie and Betsie spent ten months in three different prisons, the last being the infamous Ravensbruck concentration camp located near Berlin, Germany. Life in the camp was almost unbearable, but Corrie and Betsie spent their time sharing Jesus' love with their fellow prisoners. Many women became Christians in that terrible place because of Corrie and Betsie's witness to them. The saying in the camp was, "That's Barracks 28—the crazy place where they hope." Betsie died in Ravensbruck, but Corrie survived. The pertinent question would seem to be, what were they hoping for?

If they were hoping to be released alive from Ravensbruck, then Corrie's hopes were well placed and Betsie's were dashed.

If their hope was in Jesus Christ, whose faithfulness was sure no matter what happened, both women's hopes were met.

From all that I have read through Corrie's books, it is crystal clear that their hope was in the faithfulness and goodness of the God they loved and served.

When Corrie came home from the death camp, she determined that her life was a gift from God, and she needed to share what she and Betsie had learned in Ravensbruck with the world. One of the most remarkable treasures she mined from her time in such a dark pit she wrote about in *The Hiding Place:* "There is no pit so deep that God's love is not deeper still." She endured so much at the hands of her brutal prison guards and saw atrocities that should crush the human heart, but her love for God and her faith in Him grew and grew in the darkness of death and despair.

At age fifty-three, Corrie began a worldwide ministry that took her into more than sixty countries in the next thirty-two years! Her life message was "Jesus is victor." She died on her ninety-first birthday, April 15, 1983. It seems only fitting that Corrie's passing occurred on her birthday. In the Jewish tradition, only very blessed people are allowed the special privilege of dying on their birthdays!

As I stood outside that humble home, I imagined Corrie and Betsie as little girls running and playing together, talking to customers in their father's clock and watch shop. They could never have imagined that from such a place of love and kindness, they would be thrust into such hatred and brutality. As parents we never know what lies ahead for us or for our children, so we must live the life out of every day and tuck the truths of God's faithfulness deep into our children's hearts.

Parents can leave a shining path for their children and model a life of faith. I know that to be true because I am Elizabeth Walsh's daughter.

## ELIZABETH WALSH: WOMAN OF FAITH

For as long as I can remember, I have been surrounded by the hymns of the faith, the Word of God, and Christian family and friends. I don't know much about my father's faith firsthand, as he died when I was a child, but when I think of people who showed me what faith looks like, one of the first faces that comes to my mind is my mom's. It was clear to me even as a child that my mother had an unshakable trust in the goodness and mercy of God.

I have spoken in other books about our family story, but it has always been through my eyes and my memories. This time I asked my mom to share a little of her journey and about the death of my dad. I have not changed a word. Her words are precious to me.

My dear Sheila,

Your question to me about faith has set me thinking and turning back in my mind to many years ago when my journey to faith first began. As you know I was blessed by having Christian parents and Christian grandparents and raised in an evangelical Baptist church, so believing the Bible came naturally. But when did my own faith begin? At the age of fifteen, I was challenged about the need to make a personal commitment to Jesus, and this I did. I joined the church and also the Christian Endeavor Society (a Bible study club) and had many wonderful times of blessing and fellowship with many Christian friends. Did I find it hard to be a Christian in these early days? Not at all! It was a joy. Nothing had ever happened to really test my faith.

As you know, I met your dad, who was also a believer, and we got married and set up home. God blessed us with a daughter—your sister Frances—and two years later, we were again blessed when you came along. When, three and a half years later, Stephen, our son, was born, our joy was complete. We had the family that we had prayed for. Three healthy children: God had been good.

Who could have foreseen what was about to happen? When Stephen was one week old, I was allowed home from hospital. Christmas was just eight days away. On the morning of Boxing Day (the day after Christmas) your dad had a massive heart attack. How could this happen to a man thirty-four years of age? All I could do was pray that God would heal him. For a few days he did seem to be making progress, and then in the early hours of the fifth of January, your dad suffered a massive stroke as a result of a cerebral thrombosis. His right arm and leg were paralyzed, and he was no longer able to speak. The specialists in the hospital gave me no hope of his recovery—they were sure he would die that night. But they were not relying on the Divine Physician who can do anything.

We contacted so many people and asked for their prayers. Was I worried? I was concerned for what your dad was experiencing, but I knew that God performs miracles and He would, wouldn't He? People rallied round—baby-sitting when I was at the hospital each day, providing transport and helping in more ways than I can list. But the miracle didn't happen. God did not restore your dad to his health and strength again. He got to come home from hospital for a time, after a few months. It's hard to relate but he had no means of communicating—there was such an area of his brain that had been damaged.

Did I lose my faith over this? No, I held on tight to the Lord. I needed Him as never before. I'm not saying it was easy; nothing could be further from the truth. Having to wash him, dress him, shave him, accompany him back and forth on hospital visits, trying to get him to do the exercises for the speech therapy program, not to mention looking after a baby and two little girls, provide meals, and run a home—I was so exhausted some days that I hardly had the energy to undress at bedtime.

But God was always there for me. He gave me the strength, the patience, the ability to cope, and the faith to believe that He was in the situation with me.

But while God was there, so was the evil one. I vividly remember one night—it had been a particularly hard day and I was too tired to sleep. Around one in the morning the temperature in the bedroom suddenly dropped like a stone. I felt an evil presence in the room. As clearly as if it was audible, I heard a voice say; "Frank's not going to get better. Everyone is tired of praying for him and for you. No one is praying for you now."

No one? Surely my close friends? Surely my mother? But my grandmother not praying for me? Never! Never! Never! My grandmother was a saint, and she and I were very close. I knew that if the unthinkable happened and everyone else in the world had stopped praying for us, she hadn't. I said aloud, "Satan, you are the father of lies, and you are so wrong. In Jesus' name I command you to leave me!"

Immediately the temperature in the room returned to normal. Secure in God's peace, I slept. That was my unforgettable experience of a satanic attack, and God proved that He was the victor.

When your dad died a year later, it was a heartbreaking time which still brings tears to my eyes. I asked God then for two things: that I would live to see you all grow up and find your place in the world, and most importantly, that you would all have a faith in Jesus. God graciously answered my wishes, and it has been my joy to see each of you become Christians.

The years that have passed have been full of all kinds of situations—mountaintops and valleys, good times and bad. I've realized that God always answers our prayers, but not always as we would wish. My faith has grown stronger as the years have passed. In the best of times and in the worst of times, He is faithful and He awards our faith with blessings that we neither expect nor deserve. In the words of the old hymn, "My faith it is an oaken staff, O let me on it lean."

I know that my times are in His hands and nothing will happen to me that He does not allow.

Thank you, faithful God.
Love from Mum

P.S. Your dad would have been so proud of each of you.

My heroes are not the kind movies are made of, but they are the kinds that change lives. I thank God for the women He has placed on my path to encourage and strengthen me when I am tired and discouraged. When I see their faithfulness to God, it calls me to be faithful too.

> My faith, it is an oaken staff,
> O let me on it lean!
> My faith, it is a trusty sword,
> May falsehood find it keen!
> Thy Spirit, Lord, to me impart,
> O make me what Thou ever art,
> Of patient and courageous heart,
> As all true saints have been.
> —Thomas Lynch, 1800s

# CHAPTER 12

# WHEN FAITH IS PUT TO THE TEST

## *When God Seems Far Away*

⌒

*Abide with me: fast falls the eventide;*
*The darkness deepens; Lord, with me abide.*
*When other helpers fail, and comforts flee,*
*Help of the helpless, O abide with me!*
*I need Thy presence every passing hour:*
*What but Thy grace can foil the tempter's power?*
*Who like Thyself my guide and stay can be?*
*Through cloud and sunshine, O abide with me!*
—Henry F. Lyte, 1847

*Consider it pure joy, my brothers, whenever you face*
*trials of many kinds, because you know that the test-*
*ing of your faith develops perseverance. Perseverance*
*must finish its work so that you may be mature and*
*complete, not lacking anything.*

—James 1:2–4

*J* walked into a travel agent's office in London and said, "I've got this much money, and I want to go as far away as possible. Do you have any suggestions?"

The girl behind the desk, in a crisp white blouse and black skirt, began to flip through brochures. "What about Africa?" she asked. "Does that interest you at all?"

"Absolutely!" I said. "Which part of Africa?"

"Tunisia," she replied. "It's in the north. With that amount of money, you can stay in a nice hotel in a little town called Hammamat. How does that sound?"

"It sounds just great," I replied.

I was twenty-five years old and working for British Youth for Christ on a very minimal salary, which explains why I was being offered a package tour to someplace no one had ever heard of. That didn't matter to me. I wanted to go somewhere far away from all my friends and family, and just be alone with God for a while.

I felt trapped by my life. I knew that I wanted to serve God. I knew that I loved Him, but it seemed to me that I had relinquished any control over my life to others. I was such a people pleaser that I wasn't sure I was doing what God had called me to or what other people thought I should be doing.

Before I graduated from London Bible College, the principal, Gilbert Kirby, talked to me about staying in the mainstream of what God was doing. He said that there would always be people who wanted to sidetrack me into some little division of the kingdom, some little *holy huddle.* But he said God had not made me for that. I loved and respected that man so much, and through my time at LBC he had shared such grace and wisdom with me.

I remember striding into his office one day after a lecture on Henry VIII of England and the battle that took place during his reign between the Catholic and Protestant churches. "I'm leaving!" I announced.

"You are?" he said. "Perhaps you would like a cup of tea before you go?"

"That would be lovely," I said.

After we had enjoyed a cup of tea and played with his dog, F. F. Bruce, he asked me why I was leaving.

"The whole world is going to hell, and I'm sitting in the classroom studying some old fat guy who has been dead for years. How will that save the world?"

I thought at the time that Mr. Kirby coughed, but in retrospect I think he was laughing.

"That's a good point," he said. "I don't think I've ever thought of it quite like that before. So, do you feel ready to go out there and save the world?"

"Well . . . I'm not really ready, but I'm very willing."

"That's good. 'Willing.' That's very good," he replied. "I'm just wondering if there is any way we could help you become a little more prepared."

"I suppose there is nothing wrong with being a little more prepared," I said. "After all, I have paid my fees for the rest of the year, so it would be bad stewardship to leave now, don't you think?"

"Good point," he said. "I hadn't even thought of that. I think you're right. Just stick it out for the rest of the year, and then go out and . . . save the world."

As I think back on that conversation, I could just crawl under a rug. I was so sure of myself and so dismissive of others who didn't seem to be on fire for God. Gilbert, with grace, wisdom, and love, gently put me back on track without my even feeling the bumps.

As I was writing this book I received an e-mail from his daughter, Ruth, telling me that in 2004 her mother turned eighty and her dad would turn ninety in September. She asked if I would write a few lines for a memory book she was preparing for them.

Her note made me stop and think. It took me back through the years to a place where I felt safe and loved. There was something so comforting about being cared for by a couple like Gilbert and Connie Kirby. I'm sure Gilbert had to listen to hundreds of indignant students over the years, as he tried to graciously steer us back on track. The thing I remember most about him was that no matter what came out of my mouth when I was with him, whether it was wit or folly, he never made me feel foolish. He let me talk, get it all out of my system, and then it was as if he spread a map out before me of the greatness and faithfulness of our God. I always left his office feeling closer to Jesus. (I have a sneaking suspicion that after talking with me, he felt as if he needed a nap.)

## My Road to Tunisia

It seems as if the Christian community is divided into two groups. There are those like Gilbert and my mom who, with open arms, speak of the grace and mercy of God. They call you to His side just by the love they show. Then there are those who feel it is their job to make you toe the line, behave, and live a safe, contained life.

After I graduated from London Bible College I joined European Youth for Christ. I mentioned in the last chapter that I was based in Holland but traveled all over Europe, singing and speaking with Oasis. At the end of my time with EYFC, I returned to the United Kingdom and after a short break began working with British Youth for Christ. I loved what I did. I was part of a team that went into high schools, where we performed concerts and talked about faith issues with the students. I found it very rewarding, but a part of me was not engaged.

At times I felt motivated to find new ways of communicating my faith, but I was always told to stick to the schedule. I never wanted to upset anyone or rock the boat, so I let ideas and fresh vision fall by the wayside. I could have spoken up, but I was so locked into my own little safe world, afraid of what others might think or even what God might ask of me if I lived with real abandon and passion. I kept pushing myself to work harder and harder until I was exhausted, so I decided to do the thing that was farthest away from my comfort zone.

"I've got this much money and I want to go as far away as possible. Do you have any suggestions?"

So I had my tickets and my passport and two weeks' leave. I was going by myself, and I had no idea what to expect. I called Mom to tell her that I would be out of the country for a couple of weeks.

"Are you off to Europe?" she asked.

"Not quite Europe," I said.

"So you're just staying in the country but having a little break. That will be good for you," she replied. "You work too hard."

"Well, I'll be in *a* country, just not this country," I said.

"Oh, where are you off to, somewhere fun?"

"Yes. I'm going to Africa."

Silence.

More silence.

"Africa! Africa! What are you going to Africa for?" she asked.

"I need to think."

"Can't you think in Scotland?"

"I don't think so, Mom."

## AFRICA, HERE I COME!

As the plane began its descent into the Tunis airport, I looked out the window at the fascinating landscape below. I had never been to Africa before. All I knew about Tunisia was that it was an Arab nation, and most of the people spoke Arabic. I didn't think that would be a problem, as I didn't want to talk to anyone; I wanted to pray. I collected my bag from the luggage that was piled up in the baggage claim area and headed outside. It was springtime, and the weather was beautiful. I loved the bustle of all the people around me and the strange language.

The travel agent had told me where to catch a bus for Hammamat, so I waited at the bus stop beside a woman with a chicken in her arms. She said something to me in Arabic, and I just smiled and shrugged my shoulders, hoping that I had not just bought the chicken. It took quite a while to get to the hotel where I would be staying; we seemed to stop at every corner. At one stop the bus driver got out and went into a house. We sat and waited for about thirty minutes until he reappeared. Apparently he had gone home for lunch! Eventually the bus pulled up outside a little hotel, and the driver turned and pointed at me. "You! You! You go!"

I grabbed my bag, said good-bye to the chicken, and got out of the bus. I checked into the hotel and was given my room key. My room felt very different from any hotel room I had stayed in before. It was small and simple with very bright colors on the walls and on the bed. The floor was made out of red tile that felt cool underfoot. I sat on the edge of the bed and suddenly felt very far away from home.

"Father, I'm here because I want to hear Your voice. You know that I love You, but sometimes I feel so lost and so alone. I know that You have a plan for my life, but what if I miss it? What if I end up listening to what other people think I should do and miss You completely? If I am right in the middle of Your will, shouldn't I feel it? Because sometimes I don't. I wish You would just write me a letter and tell me exactly what to do, because I would do it."

I checked the mail the next morning and unfortunately, there was no mail with a celestial postmark. One of the things I have come to understand about my relationship with God is that I don't always get to *feel* His presence. I don't get to see the blueprints for my life; I am called to walk by faith. As a young woman sitting on the end of a bed in North Africa, I wanted what many of us want: clear direction at every turn. I wanted to know that God saw me. If I could just tune in to His Spirit, I would never take a wrong turn. The trouble with that belief is that it placed so much importance on me, on my being able to get it all right.

One of the students at seminary asked me to meet with him in the prayer chapel one morning. I knew who he was, as we had been in some social groups together, but I didn't know him well. He told me that God had shown him I was to be his wife. I was shocked! "How do you know that?" I asked.

"God speaks to me," he said. "He speaks very clearly."

"Don't you think He would speak to me too?" I asked.

"He calls you to be an obedient handmaiden," he said.

"I don't even really know you," I said.

"We will learn to know each other through prayer," he announced and handed me a small head scarf.

"What's this for?" I asked.

"It is for you to cover your head while I pray."

Well, that did it for me. Did I think it was possible that God could speak to one person about a relationship before the other? I thought that was possible. Would I find my partner for life while at seminary? I hoped I might, but would God ask me to marry someone who made me wear a red head scarf every time he prayed? Not a chance!

When I made it clear that I wasn't open to a relationship with him, he told me that I had just missed God's best for my life and everything from then on would be a poor substitute. (Incidentally, I saw him a few days later with a different girl in tow, wearing the red head scarf. I guess God changed His mind.)

Even though I didn't believe the proclamation from that earnest young man, I did live under a hybrid of that thought pattern: *What if I miss God? Will bad things happen to me because I am not in the center of His will?*

It's interesting that I spent so long as a student of God's Word and missed two of the most prevalent themes: the sovereignty of God and His faithfulness to His children at all times. When we began looking at faith together at the beginning of this book, I contrasted two friends who were experiencing very different answers to their prayers. Brandon, the young man in the car crash, is getting better and stronger and stronger every day. Janice, in her fight with cancer, is getting weaker and weaker. What is God doing here? Does God show partiality to one child over another? Does He protect some more than others?

Something was about to happen in Tunisia that would impact my life forever. I was going to find myself in a very dangerous situation where only God could help me. At almost the same time, a young woman who would become a friend of mine twenty years later was in the same situation. God was going to deliver one of us from the terror and allow the other one to walk through it.

## A DANGEROUS NIGHT

I spent most of my days walking by the beach and praying. I enjoyed the quiet and the solitude. Someone who worked for the hotel hooked me up one day with two Bedouins (Arabs who live in caves in the desert), who took me on a trip across part of the Sahara desert on a camel. The sunrise over the Sahara is one of the most spectacular sights on earth. It's as if every grain of sand suddenly catches fire and comes alive. My camel didn't seem too impressed, though, and kept spitting at me. I thought the camel was threatening, but it was nothing compared to what lay just ahead.

Soon it was almost time for me to fly home. A young man who worked with the hotel asked if on my last night I would like to eat out at a local restaurant and taste more traditional fare than the hotel served. I wasn't sure at first, but he seemed like a nice guy and he spoke perfect English. I reasoned that since he worked for the hotel, he must be okay. I was very naïve.

We met that night in the lobby and went out to his car. We drove to a small restaurant just outside of Hammamat. The food was wonderful, and there was live music too. He talked about his plans to go to America someday. I told him that I had visited once and loved it. It was a nice evening.

On the drive back to the hotel, he asked if I would like to see inside a real Tunisian home. I thought that would be lovely. It didn't cross my mind that this was not a wise choice. As I have said, I was a very naïve girl. I was twenty-five years old, and I was a virgin; I intended to stay that way until I found the right person to marry.

We drove farther out of town, and he pulled into the driveway of a small house. He opened the car door for me, and we went inside. He asked if I would like a glass of wine. I told him that I didn't drink but would love some coffee. He poured himself some wine and went into the kitchen, I assumed, to make some coffee. I had my back turned, looking at some pictures on his wall, when he came up behind me, grabbed me, and threw me down on the sofa.

## COMPASSION ABUSED

A few thousand miles away in Southern California, another story was unfolding in the life of a woman who would later become a friend of mine. Out of respect for my friend's privacy I will refer to her in this story as Sarah. Sarah wanted to go out on a date with a young man she was working with. Her mom and dad were uncomfortable with the idea as he was quite a bit older than Sarah. This man had experienced tragedy in his family and, as Sarah is a very compassionate person, she was drawn into his story. She was also a virgin and, like me, committed to remain that way until she met God's choice for her life. After some discussion Sarah persuaded her parents to allow her to have dinner with him. They had no way of knowing what the events of that night held for their daughter.

## GOD'S INTERVENTION

I was stunned as I felt strong arms push me down into the sofa. In a moment I realized how foolish I had been. I was in a house in North Africa. No one on the planet knew that I was there alone with a virtual stranger. In that moment I cried out to God to help me. I told the man who had my arms pinned to my side that I needed to tell him something. He released his grip enough to let me turn around and face him.

I spoke to him with my voice trembling. "I am so sorry if I misled you tonight. I don't do this kind of thing. I am a virgin, and I am a Christian. Please let me go back to my hotel."

He looked at me and laughed. Then he did the strangest thing. He stood, zipped up his pants, got his car keys, and went to the door. I followed him. We drove in silence to the hotel, and I got out. He drove away. I went up to my room and threw myself on the bed and wept and wept. I felt so foolish and so scared and so grateful to God. I don't have a shadow of a doubt that God orchestrated my deliverance. I am sure the man drove back to his house thinking, *Why on earth did I just do that?*

## A DREAM DESTROYED

Sarah enjoyed her date. She listened to and sympathized with this man who had seen so much trouble, and then it was time to go home. But instead of taking her home, he raped her.

Sarah is a believer. She cried out to God to deliver her, but He didn't. Why? Why would God spare me and not spare her? I wish I had a nice, tidy little answer that I could give you, but I don't. What I do know, though, is this: Sarah is now a social worker and counselor. She sits with rape victims and knows what they are feeling because she has been there. She is being used in remarkable ways to bring hope and healing to other women. She is a strong, godly woman who has walked through fire and held the hand of Christ in the midst of it.

"Consider it pure joy, my brothers, whenever you face trials of many kinds, because you know that the testing of your faith develops perseverance. Perseverance must finish its work so that you may be mature and complete, not lacking anything" (James 1:2–4). God redeems our pain and sorrow. Nothing that has happened to us is lost in His hands.

The loaves-and-fishes principle works here too. When we offer the painful things in life to God, He is able to bless them and bring hope and life to others through our brokenness. I know that Sarah would not have chosen this path for her life, but when she looks into the eyes of a young woman who has been raped, she can reach out with the compassion of one who has been there.

## MY THORN

I have struggled with clinical depression for many years; I have been on medication for twelve. Once or twice during that time I have tried unsuccessfully to come off the meds. At the beginning of 2004, I decided it was time for me to be free of the pills forever. I didn't do it foolishly and attempt to "cold-turkey" it, but I talked to my psychiatrist and we came up with a plan to reduce the dose over two weeks.

For the first month after I was off them, I felt wonderful. I felt more alive and was rid of the annoying dry mouth side effect of the drug. Then I felt myself begin to spiral down. It's hard for me to describe to you what it feels like if you have never suffered from depression. It's not like having a bad day or feeling fed up with your life. It's actually quite alarming—it feels as if a cold winter is settling in on your soul. It's hard to think clearly, to concentrate, or to be around other people.

I have been a part of Women of Faith since 1996, and I always look forward to the beginning of the new season. But in January and February of 2004, I found myself dreading it. I didn't want to get on a plane and go anywhere. I just wanted to be left alone. I thought about going back on my medication, but I didn't want to. I wanted to be "fixed," so I tried to fight through the sadness and confusion in my heart. I asked God to help me make it through the fog of despair.

One night at dinner, Christian asked if he could drink his soda out of the can. I said he could if he was careful not to spill it. He reached out to get a piece of bread, and his sleeve caught the edge of the can and it spilled all over the table.

"I told you that would happen!" I said.

"I'm so sorry, Mom," he said.

I looked into his eyes and saw something there I had never seen before. I excused myself and went into the bedroom. I sat on the floor and cried and cried. It might not seem like much to you, but Christian is a very sensitive boy. He is a good boy, and I had never raised my voice to him before. He looked so wounded and so stunned by my tone. When I had pulled myself together enough to talk, I picked up my cell phone and called my doctor's office. I left a message that I needed to see him the next day.

I never want to see that look in my son's eyes again. I lay on the floor for a while, and then I noticed a piece of paper by the door. It said,

Dear Mom,
I love you and I hope you get better soon.
I think you are a great mom,

Love,
Christian

I carry that note with me everywhere I go. Even as I read it again today, I wept. I will never again let my desire to be "fixed" be more important than being the mom that I want to be, or the speaker and writer that I am called to be. Once I got back on the medication, within a couple of weeks I was back to myself and looking forward to another year of sharing God's grace and love with thousands of women across the country.

At every conference I hear someone say, "I am so grateful that you share your experience with depression. It gives me hope. The fact that you still take your little blue pill makes me feel that I'm not alone, and that I don't have to be ashamed."

I don't always understand why God works as He does, why He heals one and not another, why He delivers one and not another, but I do believe that He is good all the time. Our faith is tested in many ways. Sometimes we are immersed in a situation that seems hopeless, and we wonder, *God, are You there?* Sometimes He delivers us from a situation in such a miraculous way that we know it had to be God; sometimes He calls us to walk with a limp, following the One who was wounded for us.

I don't know what you have walked through or what pain you have known. I don't know where you find yourself at this moment, but I encourage you to invite Christ into the midst of your struggles and heartache. Offer your scars to the One who is scarred for you. The very wounds that seemed that they might break you will be used by God to strengthen you and to give strength to others.

CHAPTER 13

# THE REWARDS OF FAITH

## *When We Share the Heart of the Shepherd*

∾

*My hope is built on nothing less*
*Than Jesus' blood and righteousness;*
*I dare not trust the sweetest frame,*
*But wholly lean on Jesus' Name.*
*On Christ, the solid Rock, I stand,*
*All other ground is sinking sand,*
*All other ground is sinking sand.*

—Edward Mote

*For the eyes of the LORD range throughout the earth*
*to strengthen those whose hearts are fully committed*
*to him.*

—2 Chronicles 16:9

The week my manuscript was due, I logged on to check my e-mail before I wrote the final chapter. I saw that there was a note about Brandon Harris. It was titled "Final Update on Brandon."

There was such joy in that simple headline. The crisis was over, and Brandon is restored.

First there was a note from Bill Todd, a friend of the Harrises' who had been keeping us all updated on Brandon's progress. Then there were a note from Brandon's mom, Jan, a note from Brandon, and a note from his dad, Chris. I asked if I could share these excerpts with you, and they graciously agreed.

It has been a joy over these past few months to share the mercy of the Lord with you regarding Brandon's miraculous survival and equally miraculous recovery. To see him walking without any assistance and recently passing his driver's exam brings tears to your eyes. His life has been a remarkable tale of God's mercy and sovereignty.

I have mentioned to the Harrises on more than one occasion what a blessing it was to fellowship, pray, and cry with those of you living in the Nashville area and "having church" at the ICU waiting rooms at Vanderbilt hospital. It was a true reflection of what the Body of Christ is all about!

Bill

To all of you precious friends and family,

Words cannot begin to express our appreciation to all of you for how you have stood by us in prayer the past 3 months . . . So many of you . . . many we have never met. We are overwhelmed and humbled by your willingness to serve us in such an incredible way.

God has moved in such amazing ways on Brandon's behalf. He is back writing songs, playing guitar, and walking again! We are in awe every day we look at him. He will always be a reminder to us of how God can take our brokenness and put us back together even better than before. I pray that God will reach His hand down on you and bless you richly for all you have given to us.

Thank you, again. We will never be the same.
I love you all so much,
Jan

And here is vintage Brandon . . .

Family and friends, I need to thank you individually for each of your personal prayers because "word on the street" is that this survival I went through was a miracle. Not being very conscious the whole time, and being on medicine, made it very fun to the point that I don't really remember any intense pains. I have to say I actually had more fun than I've had in a long time as far as I can remember, but of course that might have been from the medicine. But anyway, I just want to thank you and send everybody back onto their regular "earth lives" and encourage them to enjoy their life in peace, and also re-notice that this "earth thing" can be very short. Spiritually, I do not want to get too detailed but I do want to say that after this traumatic experience I have started to read Romans and have found more peace in my relationship with God more than ever.

> Much Peace (and Love),
> Brandon Harris

We can never say thank you enough to all of you who stood by us, said the same prayer of faith, looked at us in the eyes and said simply, "We love you!" Look what happens when we unite in prayer. Living with Brandon is like living with a Bible character. As far as we can tell, our son is 100% healed. More than anything we praise God for his positive attitude and continued faith in a sovereign God.

> Thank you from the bottom of our hearts,
> Chris Harris

It is a wonderful thing when the body of Christ comes together in faith to stand in the gap for those who are in crisis. It says so much to those who look on. Brandon's *faith entourage* was quite the topic of conversation for a while at the hospital, as his teenage friends prayed together and sang choruses in the intensive care waiting room. Many of the people who had come to visit Brandon took time to try and encourage others who waited for news of a loved one. Christian was right in his first observation of the waiting room: "There's a lot of love here!"

Brandon, Jan, and Chris have said that they will never be the same. I understand that compelling statement. When we have walked through devastating times and found God to be our Rock and Strength in the midst of it all, we are changed. God hasn't changed; we have. He has always been that strong, that loving, that merciful, that present for us, but we never availed ourselves of all of who He is before.

It is one thing to say that the Lord is my Shepherd; it is quite another to be lost and have Him guide me home.

It is one thing to say His rod and staff, they comfort me; it is quite another to be so weak I cannot stand and have them sustain me.

I have seen that in the life of a woman I have grown to love and respect over the last year.

## LIFE INTERRUPTED

I wrote in my last book, *The Heartache No One Sees*, about Evelyn Husband, who had just joined our team as a guest speaker. I mentioned earlier in this book that her husband, Rick, was a man of faith who held devotions with his crew, an unprecedented event for NASA.

You may remember that Evelyn's husband, Rick, died on February 1, 2003, over the southern United States. The space shuttle *Challenger* and her crew perished during reentry, sixteen minutes before it was due to land. While Evelyn stood with her two children, Laura and Matthew, and waited to be reunited with Rick, he was already home.

Evelyn deeply moved me the first time she spoke at one of our events in 2003. She told her story with grace and even humor. She let us into the life they shared before Rick's tragic accident. What has struck me recently, though, is how Evelyn is being changed by the journey she is on.

She was our guest at the Fort Lauderdale conference in July of

2004. Christian loves when she brings Matthew because they get to play together. We had decided that since Fort Lauderdale is by the beach, I would rent a car for Christina, our nanny, and she could take the boys to the beach on Saturday. I bumped into Evelyn in the hotel lobby on Friday night as we were leaving to go to the arena. I just love her and went up to give her a big hug.

She grinned at me but not a sound came out of her mouth. She had completely lost her voice and was on steroids. So far they had not helped, and she could barely whisper.

"What are you going to do?" I asked.

"They have sent for a tape of one of the times that I spoke last year. They're going to show that," she whispered.

"Why don't you stay here and rest tonight?" I suggested.

"No way!" she whispered with a grin.

On Saturday morning I discovered that the tape had not arrived. I asked Mary Graham what she was going to do.

"Evelyn is going to speak," she said.

"But she doesn't have any voice. How will she do that?" I asked.

"I'm not sure, but she says it will be okay."

I thought back to the first time Evelyn was our guest. She was so nervous! But now here she was, with no voice and a quiet confidence in God.

## LIGHT IN THE VALLEY OF THE SHADOW

Evelyn took the stage and smiled warmly at our audience. She apologized that her voice was weak but asked us to promise that we would not allow that to be a distraction. As she spoke, strength and joy were in her story. She talked about Rick, but more than that, she talked about Jesus. She talked about her newfound intimacy with Christ and how precious that was to her. She told us that as a family, they waited on the runway for Rick to come home so that they could have one more family hug. She said, "One day we will get that hug, and we will be in the presence of Jesus."

As I listened to my friend, I marveled at the way God had strengthened her faith in the midst of such heartache. She shared some insight on that very well-known psalm that Max Lucado had shared with us earlier that year but brought fresh insight to the passage from her own journey.

She drew our attention to two verses:

*The LORD is my shepherd; I shall not want.*
*He makes me to lie down in green pastures;*

*Yea, though I walk through the valley of the shadow of death, I will fear no evil.* (NKJV)

Evelyn drew out one word from each verse, "makes" and "shadow."

As I thought on her comments afterward, I realized how appropriate they are for us in our journey of faith. Sometimes God allows circumstances into our lives to *make* us lie down. He has such green pastures for us, but we are so involved in everything around us we don't take time to rest with Him. A wise shepherd makes his flock rest.

Rest has always been in the plan of God for us. It is something that I have missed for a long time, but now it seems so clear. God patterned it for us. We read in Genesis that God created the earth in six days and on the seventh, He rested. God didn't rest because He was tired; He rested to reflect on what He had created, and He said that it was good.

I think we have missed the whole point about the Sabbath. I grew up in Scotland, where people still kept the Sabbath as a day set apart from others. The stores were all closed, and it was a time to meet together and worship. It used to drive me nuts as a child that I couldn't change out of my Sunday outfit, put on my jeans, and go outside and play. Here in America, believers spend Sundays differently. It is common to eat out or go to the mall. The first time I suggested that we go shopping to my mother, I thought she was going to have a coronary.

But here's what I think we've missed. It's not about whether we think it's okay to buy a newspaper on a Sunday; it's about following God's pattern. God took one day out of seven, stopped and reflected on all He had created, and saw that it was good. He calls us to take a day away from all our other concerns, to stop and see what God is doing, to reflect on all of His goodness and faithfulness and see that it is good. I believe that circumstances would not overwhelm us as much if we learned the peace and confidence that come from Sabbath rest.

Sometimes we think we have done our bit if we show up for church; then the rest of the day is ours to use as we wish. We deprive ourselves of the joy and strength that comes from taking a day to celebrate who God is. Paul wrote to the church in Thessalonica, "May our Lord Jesus Christ himself and God our Father, who loved us and by his grace gave us eternal encouragement and good hope, encourage your hearts and strengthen you in every good deed and word" (2 Thess. 2:16–17).

I am learning to reprioritize my life. I don't know what the days ahead hold for Barry, Christian, and me, but God does. His help and strength are available now for those of us who will honor His command to take one day each week and soak ourselves, heart and soul, in remembrance of Him.

I don't know what the days ahead hold for my friend Janice, but I know that she is finding her strength, minute by minute, in God's presence and in His Word. She has recently completed her stem cell replacement. Again it has been a very difficult time, with a level of pain that only a morphine pump would begin to impact. Her husband, Jim, wrote that even in the worst of times, he has seen a steely determination in Janice to fight this ravenous beast. As she walks through the valley of the shadow, the light of the very close presence of Christ is with her.

Evelyn reminded us, too, that no matter how dark things seem, we are never alone. For there to be a *shadow*, there has to be light. We may be called to walk through the valley of the *shadow* of death, but because of Jesus, it is never completely dark. The Light of the World is with us. We are not alone.

Imagine a child being taken by the hand to a vast palace and told that the greatest king in the entire world lives there. The child asks, "May I go in?"

"You may go in," the guide replies, "this is the way." He points to a dark tunnel.

The child hesitates. "It's dark in there."

"It is dark," the guide agrees as he leaves.

The child looks for a long, long time. *I would love to meet the king, but what if I get lost? What if some monster consumes me?*

Her desire to meet the king overshadows her fear, and she takes the first step into the darkness. As she walks, she sees a faint light ahead. She walks toward it. "May I walk with you?" she asks.

"It would be my joy," the voice answers.

It is still dark but not completely dark. She is still afraid but not consumed by fear. It is only when they emerge on the other side of the tunnel that the child realizes she has been walking with the King all along.

## Extraordinary Faith

Extraordinary faith comes from being in relationship with our extraordinary God. It's not about us; it's all about Him.

The writer to the Hebrews gave us an astonishing list of those who remained faithful to God through hardship, famine, and death, and they are an inspiration to us. But then he directed our gaze back to our Savior. This is one of my favorite passages of God's Word. It seems a good place to rest for a while.

> Let us fix our eyes on Jesus, the author and perfecter of our faith, who for the joy set before him endured the cross, scorning its shame, and sat down at the right hand of the throne of God. Consider him who endured such opposition from sinful men, so that you will not grow weary and lose heart. (Heb. 12:2–3)

Are you discouraged?

Are you bogged down by behaviors that consume your time and energy?

Do you wonder if your one life really makes a difference?

Take another look at Jesus! He pressed through the pain and shame of this world, knowing that soon He would sit beside his Father, having made a way for you and me to come home.

Hold on!

Take heart!

Remember who you are and where you are going!

When I am down and, oh my soul, so weary;
When troubles come and my heart burdened be;
Then, I am still and wait here in the silence,
Until you come and sit awhile with me.

You raise me up, so I can stand on mountains;
You raise me up, to walk on stormy seas;
I am strong, when I am on your shoulders;
You raise me up . . . To more than I can be.

Amen.

# CHAPTER 14

# The Adventure Continues

## *When We Walk by Faith Until We See His Face*

∽

*O come, all ye faithful, joyful and triumphant,*
*O come ye, O come ye, to Bethlehem;*
*Come and behold Him born the King of angels;*
*O come, let us adore Him,*
*O come, let us adore Him,*
*O come, let us adore Him,*
*Christ, the Lord.*

—John Wade, 1743

*Glorify the LORD with me;*
*let us exalt his name together.*
*I sought the LORD, and he answered me;*
*he delivered me from all my fears.*
*Those who look to him are radiant;*
*their faces are never covered with shame.*

—Psalm 34:3–5

"What would you think about moving to Dallas?" Barry asked me one morning in the early spring of 2004.

"Dallas? I don't have big enough hair to live in Dallas!" I replied.

"No, I'm serious, Sheila. Would you be open to that?" he asked.

"I guess," I said. "I really like living in Nashville, though."

"I do, too, but it would be good for me to be closer to the Women of Faith offices."

At the beginning of 2004, Barry and Jason Clairmont (Patsy's son) took on new responsibilities on the concourse at all our events. Instead of just taking care of their own families' book tables, they began to oversee all book tables. Barry became involved with the creative and marketing side of our events as well. This meshed with his passion to make sure that the right book or CD gets into the hands of the right woman. We want her to continue her journey long after the weekend is over. This new commitment meant that he had to fly into Dallas several weekends a year and be at the arena on Thursday evenings to help set up.

"I'm not sure Christian would be thrilled to move away from his friends," I said.

"He makes new friends very quickly," Barry reminded me.

"Our house would need to sell," I said, trying to throw one more complication into the mix.

"God knows that," he said. "Let's pray that if we are supposed to move to Dallas, our house will sell. I'll call our realtor and ask if she has any suggestions on how to make our house more sellable."

I called my mom and asked what she thought. She told me that when she visited Dallas in 2003, she had had a strong sense that we would end up there. By then I realized that this was more than just a casual idea of Barry's. I began to look at schools in the Dallas area.

Ney Bailey gave me the name of a Christian school that has a wonderful reputation for academics and the arts. I looked at the campus online and was very impressed. I called the head of admissions. We were by then very close to the school's cutoff point for new students.

"Can you send me Christian's test scores from first grade?" she asked.

"He hasn't had the test yet. They test in May in Nashville," I told her, realizing that this was one more point against us.

"I will hold a place for him for two weeks," she said. "Perhaps you can get him tested early."

I told her that I would try and thanked her for her graciousness. I tried to find a way to do that, but I couldn't get it done on time. We were on the road every weekend, and our house was still on the market with no offers. After the two weeks I said to Barry, "I need to call the school tomorrow. What do I say?"

"I think it's clear. The house is still on the market with no sign of an offer. I think we have to pass."

I called the school the next morning and talked again with the head of admissions. "It doesn't seem as if this is God's time for us to move," I said. "Our house hasn't sold, and I haven't managed to get Christian tested."

"We would love to have had you in our family, but perhaps the timing is not right. Maybe next year," she said.

I thanked her and hung up. We paid the first installment of tuition for second grade in Nashville.

## HOUSELESS

The following month the house sold, and we found ourselves in a tiny apartment. Barry began looking at houses in Nashville or lots where we could build, but nothing felt right. We waited and prayed that God would guide us. Summer came, and conferences were back-to-back. The deadline for this book hung over my head like a malnourished vulture, waiting for the beast on the road to hurry up and die.

At the end of June, Barry had meetings in Dallas, so he took Christian with him to let me finish the manuscript in peace. On June 27 they went to a baseball game with Mary and Ney. Barry called me from the ballpark. "I love it here!" he said. "I understand now what you say you miss sometimes at the end of a weekend, when we fly in one direction and our buddies fly off in another. It's community, hanging with those you love, going for ice cream or to a ball game. I could really see us here."

"Perhaps next year, babe," I said.

"I guess," he said.

All that night I couldn't sleep. I felt unsettled and excited, but I didn't know why. I got up early and took my computer to Starbucks. I opened the Bible software on my computer and read,

"The LORD had said to Abram, 'Leave your country, your people and your father's household and go to the land I will show you'" (Gen. 12:1). As I read, I felt such a stirring in my spirit.

"But Abraham didn't have a son going into second grade," I reminded the Lord. "I would be willing to go anywhere, Lord, if I knew that You were guiding us. But what about Christian? He has a place in school here in Nashville and no place in Dallas."

Just then my cell phone rang. I saw that it was a Dallas prefix so I said, "Hi, babe, how did you sleep?"

The voice was not Barry's. It was the head of admissions at the school in Texas. "I felt compelled to call you," she began. "One place has opened up in second grade. I have no idea if your house has sold, or if you are even still interested, but I knew I had to call you."

"Not only has our house sold," I told her, "Barry is in Dallas with Christian today, and he has Christian's test results with him to show to our friends!"

"Do you think you are interested?" she asked.

"Can you give me till 5:00 PM today?" I said.

After I hung up I went outside and sat on the steps. "Do You want us to go, Lord?" I asked.

It is hard to put into words how loud the reply was. I didn't hear an audible voice, but there was a boom in my spirit: "*Go!*" I very rarely have that kind of specific direction and intense awareness of God's voice.

I called Barry and told him what had just happened. Suddenly it seemed as if we had switched roles; now he was a little unsure. "Do you think we are supposed to go? It's a big move," he said. "Christian would miss his friends."

"I'm sure we are to go. Remember, he makes friends very quickly! Can you buy a house this week?"

He laughed and said that he would try, and I called the school and accepted the place that God had saved for our boy.

## A JOURNEY OF FAITH

By July 1, Barry had found and bought our home! He e-mailed a picture of it to me.

"It looks great," I said. "Does Christian like it?"

"He loves it. The guy who owns the house has five dogs. I think Christian might think they come with the house."

We cleared up that little misconception and discussed move-in dates. We discovered that we could take possession two days before school started. I flew in for the day to see what we had just purchased! Mary, Ney, and Luci met us at the house, and we went in together. As we walked from room to room, I wept at the goodness of God. The house is the perfect size, it's warm and inviting, and it's five minutes away from Mary, Ney, and Luci. I stood in the guest powder room and looked at a special little touch that I believe God placed there just for me. Instead of a regular faucet, the water pours from a lion's head. I have always treasured the picture of Christ as the Lion of Judah. When I lived in England, a friend and poet, Stuart Henderson, wrote a moving piece that encourages all who love God to bury their faces in the mane of the Lion of Judah.

This all took place on July 4, 2004, my first Independence Day as an American citizen. Since the following day was my birthday, Mary, Ney, and Luci took the three of us out for a celebration lunch before we flew back to Nashville to pack—again! We talked about the journey that God has had us all on over the last ten years. There have been wonderful times and sad times, births and deaths, laughter and tears. The constant thread has been and continues to be the faithfulness of God. Only God could take me from a scared little girl who kept her heart tightly contained to a woman who believes with *all* her heart that God is faithful. No matter what happens to shake my world, underneath are the everlasting arms.

## The Journey Continues

As we flew home that night, Barry and I marveled at how far God had brought us since we first met. I asked if he remembered the conversation we had had eight years before on the hillside across from the little house we were renting in Southern California. I had asked him one evening,

"If you could do anything you wanted, babe, what would it be?"

"I would want us to work together," he said. "But I would want to be involved behind the scenes, and I would want our baby with us."

"Me too," I said. "But I have no idea what that would be."

A few days later I received a phone call from Steve Arterburn, a friend of many years.

"Sheila, I want you to consider joining a team of women who have begun to travel together. They are called Women of Faith."

"I can't do that, Steve. I'm pregnant," I told him.

"You could bring the baby," he said. "Would Barry be willing to travel with you?"

"But I wouldn't fit. What if they knew that I had spent a month in a psychiatric ward?" I asked.

"I think you'd like these women," he said. "Would you meet them?"

I walked into Steve's office in Laguna Beach, California, and said hello to Luci Swindoll, Marilyn Meberg, and Barbara Johnson. I looked into their eyes, and I knew that God had given Barry and me the desire of our hearts. I had found a place to call home with other women who didn't have life all neatly wrapped up with a bow on top, but whose absolute trust is in the faithfulness and goodness of God.

So as I bring this book to a close, a new adventure lies ahead for our family. We are grateful to be living so close to our friends when our Scottish family is so far away. Christian has known these women all his life. They are foundation stones in his path. In his prayers now he thanks God that he gets to live beside family.

I have a message saved on my cell phone. It came in on the evening of July 4 as we were flying home to Nashville: "Hi, honey, it's Luci. I just wanted to say if you need anything, any encouragement, anything at all, just call."

Luci's words echo the heart of God the Father to us, for this is what our God offers us right now. Wherever you are in life, no matter what is going on, whether you are in the best days or the worst days of your life, God loves you and will faithfully walk with you through it all.

This is what is extraordinary about faith to me: God takes fragile, flawed human hearts, with all their hopes and fears and doubts, and weaves His goodness and strength into them. Only God could do that!

> He makes my feet like the feet of a deer;
>    he enables me to stand on the heights. (Psalm 18:33)

# EPILOGUE

∽

When we began this journey together I laid out four events that at the time seemed unrelated and yet they all cast a shadow over what I was writing.

1. Grand larceny in San Jose
2. An unexpected e-mail
3. A devastating car crash
4. The great uprooting

Well, I never did recover my computer, but I'm really glad about that. What I did discover was the original folder I was using while writing the third of the book that was on the stolen computer. As I re-read my notes I found myself thinking I had come to conclusions about faith too quickly. Faith remains a mystery to me. At times God gives us the kind of faith and assurance so that we are absolutely certain about the steps we are taking. At other times we walk along a dimly lit path, our only hope being that if we take a wrong turn, God will show us.

Janice continues her relentless battle with cancer. She waits, as I write, for a bone-marrow transplant. Sometimes when I think of Janice I think of the day that my West Highland terrier first put his paws in snow. He had no idea what it was but he took the fist step and then the next and the next. His progress was slow, but each paw print left a mark. That is how I think of Janice. She is in uncharted territory, and her steps are slow, but each one that she takes by faith leaves a mark for those who are watching and for those who come behind.

Brandon Harris continues to be a teenage boy, which is just about the best thing you could say! His recovery is remarkable in every way. He has set all sorts of hospital records and is loving and living his life.

Barry, Christian, Belle, and I are now firmly ensconced in Texas. We have added a hamster to our family unit and are working on a drawl to our speech.

If you would permit me, I would like to leave you with just one thing. I don't know how you feel you measure up in the "faith" stakes, but I pray with all my heart that you will know in the depth of your soul that you are loved by God, right now, just as you are. I pray that we will all learn to walk before God with open hands—for faith is a gift after all!

# About the Author

*If* anyone is surprised by joy, it's **Sheila Walsh**. She's been successful in many areas—as a speaker, author, singer, and television talk show host. But she also knows what it is to battle depression and even contemplate suicide. It has been through the light and the darkness that God has taught her about his love. Today, she shares that love through her speaking and writing. Sheila is author of the award-winning *Gigi, God's Little Princess* series for girls (Retailers' Choice 2006) as well as multiple books for women, including *The Heartache No One Sees*, *Extraordinary Faith*, and *I'm Not Wonder Woman*. Sheila lives in Frisco, Texas, with her husband, Barry, and son, Christian.

## Acknowledgments

Sheila would like to thank,

- Mike Hyatt. Mike you are a brilliant leader. You are a visionary who believes in the power of the written word to impact the hearts and souls of those who are hungry to know God. Thank you for listening to our Father's heart.

- Jonathan Merkh. Jonathan, God has knit together your brilliant gifts and your tender heart, and your life makes a difference.

∞ Brian Hampton. I am more indebted to you than I can say. You have graciously guided me through this project amidst many obstacles. Your patience and wisdom have touched my life. You have sifted through my thoughts and ideas and brought them into focus, and I am very grateful.

∞ Kyle Olund. Kyle, once again your careful consideration of the text has fine-tuned this project so that those who have ears to hear will be able to do so clearly. Thank you for your invaluable input.

∞ Sealy Yates and the staff at Yates and Yates. Vessels would be left adrift without a skilled captain at the helm. Thank you for the years of experience and care that you bring to my life.

∞ Mary Graham. Mary, together we have watched as God moved in ways we could not have imagined. As thousands of women have flooded into the kingdom of God, we have wept together and blessed God's name that we were born for such a time as this.

∞ Patsy Clairmont, Nicole Johnson, Marilyn Meberg, Luci Swindoll, and Thelma Wells. You are family to me. I love and treasure you. You make me laugh and cry, sing and dance, and rest easier in this world just knowing that you are my friends.

∞ The staff of Women of Faith. I can't believe that this is our tenth anniversary of being part of God's heart through Women of Faith. What a joy and gift to serve with you all.

∞ Barry and Christian. What can I say! We share our lives, our hopes and dreams and our dog and our hamster! I love you both more than I can say. I am a blessed woman—Barry, to be your wife, and Christian, to be your mom.

# GOD HAS A

## *Dream*

## FOR YOUR LIFE

"*I believe* that God wants to teach us how to dream again. I believe too that he wants to fulfill our dreams. It might not be in the way we anticipate, but if we are open to his heart, this great adventure will change us. It's a risky business to dream, for dreaming leaves us open to disappointment. But I think that when we stop dreaming, a part of us dies. So I say it's time to dream again, knowing that with God, nothing is impossible! Perhaps like Dorothy and Toto we might be in for the ride of our lives!"

In *God Has a Dream for Your Life*, Sheila uses stories from *The Wizard of Oz*, World Vision, her family, and the Bible to help women catch a vision for God's love for them and His desire to work through them, freeing them to dream again.

Hardcover ISBN 10: 0-8499-0133-2
ISBN 13: 978-0-8499-0133-1

# WOMEN OF FAITH®

Women of Faith®, North America's largest women's conference, is an experience like no other. Thousands of women — all ages, sizes, and backgrounds — come together in arenas for a weekend of love and laughter, stories and encouragement, drama, music, and more. The message is simple. The result is life-changing.

*What this conference did for me was to show me how to celebrate being a woman, mother, daughter, grandmother, sister or friend.*
*— Anne, Corona, CA*

*I appreciate how genuine each speaker was and that they were open and honest about stories in their life—even the difficult ones.*
*— Amy, Fort Worth, TX*

*GO, you MUST go. The Women of Faith team is wonderful, uplifting, funny, blessed. Don t miss out on a chance to have your life changed by this incredible experience.*
*— Susan, Hartford, CT*